28 Business Thinkers Who Changed the World

The management gurus and mavericks who changed the way we think about business

RHYMER RIGBY

KoganPage

LONDON PHILADELPHIA NEW DELHI

First published in Great Britain and the United States in 2011 by Kogan Page Limited

120 Pentonville Road	1518 Walnut Street, Suite 1100	4737/23 Ansari Road
London N1 9JN	Philadelphia PA 19102	Daryaganj
United Kingdom	USA	New Delhi 110002
www.koganpage.com		India

© Rhymer Rigby, 2011

The right of Rhymer Rigby to be identified as the author of this work has been asserted by him in accordance with the Copyright, Designs and Patents Act 1988.

ISBN	978 0 7494 6239 0
E-ISBN	978 0 7494 6240 6

British Library Cataloguing-in-Publication Data
A CIP record for this book is available from the British Library.

Library of Congress Cataloging-in-Publication Data
Rigby, Rhymer.
 28 business thinkers who changed the world : the management gurus and mavericks who changed the way we think about business / Rhymer Rigby.
    p. cm.
 ISBN 978-0-7494-6239-0 -- ISBN 978-0-7494-6240-6 1. Businesspeople--Biography. 2.
Management. 3. Business. I. Title. II. Title: Twenty eight business thinkers who changed the world.
 HC29.R54 2011
 338.092'2--dc22
                                        2011000191

Typeset by Saxon Graphics Ltd, Derby
Print production managed by Jellyfish
Printed and bound in Great Britain by CPI Antony Rowe

Contents

Introduction
What makes a great business thinker?

One description of Rupert Murdoch isn't a bad first answer – it's 'the ability to consistently see round the corner'. But actually the more you look the more you realize that defining what makes a real game changer is about as easy as nailing jelly to a wall. In many cases, you can fairly accurately distil what these people did into a sentence or less. Ingvar Kamprad: brought style to the masses. Warren Buffett: invested in what he understood and believed in. Anita Roddick: business for social change. Howard Schultz: coffee as a lifestyle statement. And so on. But it doesn't really help that much.

Perhaps then they did something startlingly original or something that was blindingly obvious but only in hindsight. Sometimes this is the case. For instance, Mary Kay Ash's great USP was that her business offered women the chances denied to them elsewhere. Sometimes people find a new way of doing what already exists. Google certainly wasn't the first search engine, but it was much, much better than those that came before it. But sometimes people are not really original at all. Ray Kroc did not come up with the original McDonald's concept, nor was his the first restaurant chain. And, as the regular comparisons to Hearst suggest, Rupert Murdoch is hardly the first tycoon to see the possibilities of media ownership and power.

What you realize eventually is that although you can pull together a list of attributes that are likely to make a businessperson go from everyday success to the kind of success that changes a sector, and sometimes even the world, there is no magic list of ingredients. In an entertainingly scathing book review published in 1987, PJ O'Rourke, wrote: 'They are America's young management meatballs. And every man jack of them has a copy of *Iacocca: A Biography* under his arm... The secret is in there. The meatball knows it. If he can just read carefully enough, he'll crack the code.' O'Rourke made no secret of his contempt for Iacocca, describing him a few lines later as 'a conceited, big-mouth glad-handing huckster'. But he made a more serious point too – and one that's so obvious as to be often ignored. Most of the time, the secret of someone's success is that there is no secret. Or rather the secret is so obvious that it's not really a secret at all.

Of course, any list like this will to some extent be arbitrary. It's like a top 100 list of films or songs or books. Outside a kind of universal core, you can always make an argument that X should have been left off and Y should have been put on – and there will be people who are marginal cases. Here the criterion has simply been that, in some way or another, **these people are game changers who had significant and lasting effect on the world of business – and sometimes even the world.**

This gives a rather broad remit and has even led to the inclusion of one man who was more an academic than anything else, Tim Berners-Lee. That said, as he was the man behind the world wide web, it's not difficult to argue that he has changed the business landscape – and for virtually everyone in the world. Of course, there's a limit to this kind of reasoning. Make the criteria too wide and you have to start including politicians, artists and so on. But Berners-Lee stays because he directly changed the business world. This kind of reasoning is true, to a lesser extent, of people like Anita Roddick. There are individuals who built up far larger business empires who have not made the cut, but she was the first to fuse business and ethical concerns in a way that appealed to the mainstream – and in doing so she had an impact on the world out of all proportion to the size of her business.

The list also has a strong US bias, but that shouldn't surprise anyone. The 20th century – the century in which the modern world of business was made – has been largely a US century. And most of the business world's seismic changes, from automation to outsourcing to the dotcom revolution and the financial crisis, have had their genesis in the United States. For nearly 100 years, the greatest concentration of wealth and entrepreneurial talent the world has ever seen has been American. Had this book been published in 1911, it would probably have been dominated by the British; and were it to be published 100 years hence, Indian and Chinese businesspeople could well dominate.

There's another reason too. It is perhaps the nature of Anglo-Saxon capitalism that leads it to produce so many influential people. Capitalism as practised in the United States has two notable attributes that set it apart. Firstly, it's very winner-takes-all. This tends to produce highly visible heroic figures who are venerated above all because they represent, more or less, the capitalist American dream. Places like Europe and Japan do have their hugely influential businesspeople, but they tend to be far lower-key, and there is a far more consensual, collegiate culture (Britain, as ever, sits somewhere in the middle). US capitalism is also extraordinarily disruptive, especially when compared to somewhere like Japan. Old paradigms die quickly, and new ones rise to take their place. Again, this tends to produce heroic figures. These factors are both strengths and weaknesses, but capitalism practised this way does tend to throw up more iconic figureheads than its other variants.

If it's hard to pick game changers by their actions, then what about trying to pin down their attributes? For instance, one might expect that, to be a great business thinker, you need to be extraordinarily clever. And there's no doubt that some of them are – especially those in clever industries. The Google duo, Bill Gates and Steve Jobs are all undoubtedly extremely bright people. Yet being clever is not a prerequisite. The old cliché that a lot of business is not rocket science has more than a grain of truth to it. In many industries there are extremely successful individuals who probably score very highly in terms of 'emotional intelligence' but are not especially outstanding in terms of their brains. As Sir Martin Sorrell says, 'Business isn't brain surgery, is it?' (Rigby, 2004).

So too with background. It's tempting to think that the Rockefellers of our age either rose effortlessly from gilded launch pads or clawed their way up from desperate poverty. Sometimes it's true. Oprah Winfrey grew up in very difficult conditions in the Deep South, and there are those on this list who, as the saying goes, 'were born on third base'. But equally there are plenty of middle-class backgrounds out there too. Great business thinkers are drawn from all walks of life. The BBC's Robert Peston (2009) has talked about the 'entrepreneur's wound', which suggests that an awful childhood, which one is constantly running away from, can be the key to success. Again, there is some truth to this. The swashbucklingly ambitious are not necessarily happy or motivated by what could be described as healthy ambition, and their victories may well be at the expense of others. 'People who are very successful are often slightly or hugely screwed up,' says former Granada Chief Gerry Robinson (Rigby, 2004). 'Something in that drive is negative. It could be looking for something that's not there. It could be fear of failure. I mean, look at someone like Murdoch – what the hell's he doing it for? Is another deal going to make any difference? There ought to be some learning in life.'

But you can be a game changer and be well balanced. For every Sam Walton, there are people who have achieved huge success and do seem to be genuinely happy. Richard Branson is forever moving on to the next thing, yet his drive seems to be bound up in a kind of permanent cheerfulness – and others ranging from Buffett to the Google pair seem pretty happy with their lot. Nor do you have to treat people badly. Certainly there are those like Facebook's Zuckerberg who seem to leave a trail of the aggrieved, but what of

Tim Berners-Lee and Anita Roddick? They are widely held up as nice, well-balanced individuals, content with their lives. Even Bill Gates, for all his detractors, decided to become the biggest philanthropist in history.

Perhaps the most surprising thing though in our youth-centric world is the assumption that greatness always appears young. It doesn't. Ray Kroc, the man behind McDonald's, was in his 50s, in the twilight of his career, when his great opportunity came along. Mary Kay Ash, when asked how she succeeded so quickly, said, 'The answer is I was middle aged, had varicose veins and I didn't have time to fool around.' And just before his career took off David Ogilvy wrote a memo that began, 'Will Any Agency Hire This Man? He is 38, and unemployed...'

One thing that all of them do seem to have though is ambition and drive, sometimes to an extraordinary degree. A very clear example of this is Ray Kroc. It wasn't Kroc who had the original idea for the restaurant, who started the business, or even who applied the Henry Ford template to the quick-service restaurant business. But what Kroc did have was an ambition and a vision that the brothers McDonald (who did found the business) lacked. And it was this, not a catchy name or a clever system, that turned a handful of restaurants in California into one of the most recognized brands in the world. This kind of single-minded drive, says former M&S CEO Sir Richard Greenbury, cannot be manufactured: 'It's either in you or it isn't. It's part of one's character.' There is perhaps one other factor all share, and it's an appetite for risk. Most game changers – and especially the highly entrepreneurial ones – like to take risks in a way that other people just do not.

But while these things might be necessary conditions, they aren't sole conditions. In terms of external factors, there is timing, the business climate, being in the right place at the right time and any number of other factors. Who you are, people skills and political skills will certainly help you, and a certain ruthlessness is unlikely to do you any harm. A contrarian mindset doesn't hurt, and so on.

And then there's the big one. As Gerry Robinson once said to me, 'You need luck. Everyone needs a bit of luck.'

This is often rather understated – not least, one suspects, because management likes to think of itself as a real science. But a bit of good luck is crucial. Warren Buffett memorably noted that, if he'd been born in Peru or Bangladesh, he'd have probably been a subsistence farmer. But even those who come from comfortable backgrounds have usually taken a punt on the right industry at the right time somewhere along the line. What's more, you do make your own luck too. Robinson adds, 'Most people who do very well have just performed bloody well at whatever it is they were doing.' Indeed, one suspects that, for all Buffett's rather folksy modesty, if he were to find himself farming in Peru or Bangladesh, it wouldn't last long.

So are we saying that you can't learn from these people? Not at all. Business history illuminates the present and lights the path ahead. The stories of many of these people are tied into the story of the 20th century: both Grove and Soros escaped the Holocaust and made a new life in the United States. Moreover, as big business has had a greater and greater impact on the lives of everyday people, it's interesting to look at how its leading exponents have reflected the changing world and often driven that change.

On a practical level, great business thinkers have much to teach us. Those who want to be more innovative could do far worse than emulate certain aspects of the Google duo's behaviour. Those who want to learn about branding and publicity have no better model than Richard Branson. And anyone who wants to set up a socially responsible business should start reading up on Anita Roddick. But what you will not learn is *to be* one of these people. This incidentally is almost certainly how MBAs tend to be very successful, but not game changers. You can teach people a lot, but what you cannot teach people is to be someone other than who they are.

So there you have it. Hard work, risk taking, the right circumstances, a dash of luck and perhaps a couple of other items from the entrepreneur's ingredient cupboard. That's the secret, and that's all there is to it. If you have it, you probably already know it – or just do it, unthinkingly. And if you don't, well, you probably shouldn't berate yourself about it. You're probably just a well-balanced person who is successful by any normal yardstick.

References and further reading

O'Rourke, PJ (1987) The deep thoughts of Lee Iacocca (review), in *Give War a Chance*, pp 145–50

Peston, Robert (2009) *The Entrepreneur's Wound*, BBC Radio 4, 30 October

Rigby, R (2004) Naked ambition and how to get it, in *Management Today* [Online] http://www.managementtoday.co.uk/news/450123/Naked-ambition

Chapter One
Steve Jobs

If you had to pick a single individual who personified Silicon Valley, you'd have a list of contenders who would probably include Bill Hewlett and David Packard, Bill Gates (even though Microsoft is not in the Valley), Andy Grove and the Google duo. But for a lot of people, the choice would be an easy one – and they would plump for Steve Jobs. On one hand, he is the epitome of the cool geek, effortlessly blending a love and understanding of technology with a slightly alternative, left-of-field world view. And on the other, he is clearly an incredible businessman. Apple, of which he is Co-founder, Chairman and CEO, has an intuitive understanding of design and user interface that is arguably the finest of any company in the world.

Indeed Apple, which Jobs personifies, is not so much a company as a cultural phenomenon. Its product launches are 'events', its consumers have a devotion that sometimes borders on religious mania, it splits opinion sharply, and anyone with an interest in design, or just the modern consumer world, should have an interest in Apple. And for many Apple is Jobs and Jobs is Apple.

Jobs was born in 1955; his birth mother was single and he was given up for adoption. The couple who adopted him were Paul and Clara Jobs who lived in Mountain View, California. During his childhood and teens, nearby San Francisco was the capital of counterculture. But while Northern California may have been the hippy capital of the world, there was another revolution stirring nearby too. From the 1950s onward the research at Stanford University was turning Silicon Valley (the term was coined in 1971) into a global high-tech centre. Both of Northern California's 20th-century revolutions left their marks on Jobs. He is the quintessential West Coast liberal – alternative in his views and, for that matter, the way he runs his company. Yet he is also one of the most influential businesspeople of the late 20th century – and when it comes to high-end consumer electronics he is without equal.

After finishing high school in Cupertino, California, Jobs went on to study sciences – as well as literature and poetry – at Reed College in Portland, Oregon. He lasted only a term, and returned to his home town, where he found employment as a technician at Atari. Already something of a geek, he also joined the now legendary Homebrew Computer Club, where he met Steve Wozniak. A trip to India for spiritual enlightenment followed, after which he returned to Atari. In 1976, Jobs and Wozniak, along with Ronald Wayne (who is now a forgotten and rather melancholy footnote in Valley history), co-founded Apple in the Jobs family garage. The Apple I was launched in 1977, without a keyboard, case or monitor; it was priced at $666.66, or just under $2,500 in 2010 dollars, and was an immediate success.

The start-up moved quickly. In 1977, the company introduced the Apple II, and in 1979 the Apple II+. In 1980 the company went public, making Jobs worth $165 million. But it was a visit to Xerox in 1979 that really set Apple on its present path. Jobs had bought stock in the company and went to see the Xerox Alto, which was the first computer with a GUI – the graphical user interface that virtually every desktop or laptop uses today. Apple had already been working on a GUI, but what Jobs saw at Xerox spurred it on and in 1983 it launched the Apple Lisa. Internal politics were becoming a factor, and Jobs had been pushed off the Lisa project. This was no bad thing, as Lisa was a commercial flop and it led Jobs to join the Macintosh project. In 1984, the Apple Mac launched to great fanfare with the company's famed '1984' ad.

Although Jobs and Apple are considered pretty much indivisible, many people forget that he didn't last very long after the Mac's launch, and the two parted ways for over a decade. In 1985, Jobs was pushed out of Apple after a power struggle with the CEO, John Sculley. The reasons behind this were perhaps unsurprising: Jobs was brilliant and inspiring but could be temperamental and capricious, and the company was becoming more bureaucratic and corporate as it grew.

So he left to found NeXT, a computer company that is barely remembered outside geek circles. In fairness, its product, the NeXTcube, looked beautiful and it was technologically advanced – perhaps in some ways too advanced. But the main problem was its price tag – an eye-watering $6,500. As a result of this, the Cube's sales were lacklustre. In the meantime, Jobs had his fingers in other pies too. In 1986, he bought Pixar from George Lucas for $10 million. In 1995, Pixar released *Toy Story*, and then came its initial public offering – Jobs's stake was worth $585 million. But it was hard to escape the feeling that Apple and Jobs were like a great rock band whose difficult but brilliant frontman had left to pursue solo projects. They were very good apart, but nothing like what they were together.

Apple did all right until the mid-1990s, when its share price began a steep decline. In 1996 Jobs sold NeXT to Apple for $430 million, which he took in shares. The company made a loss of $816 million that year. By 1997, many were predicting its demise – a *Newsweek* story from July was typical of the view of many. The headline read: 'A death spiral: after years of decline, Apple needs a strategy – and a savior'. That saviour was the company's brilliant and difficult co-founder.

Jobs returned to Apple and put NeXT people in key positions. And although commercially speaking NeXT was a bit of a damp squib, its influence on Apple – and the computing world as a whole – was significant. Firstly, NeXT represented a big leap forward in terms of graphical interfaces. And secondly, at NeXT Jobs had created a culture that he felt was the answer to the stifling bureaucracy. Shortly after rejoining, Jobs became interim CEO; two years later, the position was made permanent.

With Jobs back at the helm, the company became focused and profitable again. He dumped a series of projects such as the Newton Handheld and concentrated on the iMac. He also began the process of diversification, which turned the company into as much a consumer electronics company as a computer seller. In 2001, the category-killing iPod music player was launched, and in 2007 the iPhone made its début – it has done much the same for mobiles. Both now comfortably outsell the company's computers. In 2010, the company launched the iPad tablet. Many were uncertain (especially as tablets have such a chequered history), but its impressive sales suggested that Apple's loyal customers were not among them. Indeed, the oft-repeated sentiment that Steve Jobs knows what you want before you want it seems to hold true.

Many said that this was all very well, but, while the iPod and iPhone have carried all before them, these devices did little to boost the sale of Macs. In addition, while the company had 4–8 per cent of the operating system market, Microsoft has never had under 90 per cent, and the Mac has made few gains outside its traditional strongholds of the creative industries and image-conscious home users. But Jobs may be one step ahead again. Increasingly people do access their phones from a broad variety of devices, so perhaps transition from computer company to digital lifestyle company is the long-term smart move.

The markets would certainly seem to agree. Perhaps because of the boutique image its products have and the anti-establishment pose it strikes, many people tend to forget just how huge Apple has become. In April 2010 it was second on the S&P 500, beaten only by Exxon Mobil (and ahead of arch-rival Microsoft). If you compare its five-year share performance with the performance of its main rivals, it is Apple that is the star. Indeed, for all its alternative posturing, Apple is a very successful and a very big business.

You find this sort of contradiction all over the company too, and you could argue that they are key to both Apple and the man who embodies it. The company portrays itself as an outsider, when it commands over 70 per cent of the MP3 player market and around 50 per cent of the mobile phone market. It affects openness, yet the lockdown it has on its products is far stronger than anything Microsoft has (with Apple you buy both the hardware and the operating system). It somehow carries a whiff of hippy values about its products, but if you want a green computer you should buy a Dell, not a Mac. And, although Jobs has said that 'innovation is what distinguishes leaders from followers', Apple has not been the originator of any one of its products. Starting with the Xerox Alto and moving on through the iPod and the iPhone, someone else has always been first. Indeed, if you had to sum up the company's strategy, it would be 'brilliant second' rather than genuine innovator.

Lest this sounds like criticism, it isn't really. The title of the 2004 book *Fast Second: How smart companies bypass radical innovation to enter and dominate new markets* says it all really. Those who dive in first often fail to fully reap the rewards of the new market they've entered. Better to be second when you've learned from your competitor's mistakes. The first MP3 player, for those who are interested, was the MPMan F10, manufactured by Korea's SaeHan Information Systems. It arrived in 1998, three years before the iPod, and others followed it. But their difficult interfaces and fiddly natures meant they were for geeks only. The iPod, on the other hand, was easy to use, and that's why it came to dominate its market. Six years later, the iPhone repeated the trick, albeit in a much more mature market. It made something functional beautiful and easy to use.

Apple's genius lies at the customer interface, not in the nuts and bolts. Jobs knows that what people want is stuff that looks beautiful and is beautifully easy to use. Most people don't care about openness (as with the iPhone) or raw performance figures (as with the Mac's processors) or even sound quality (the iPod is probably not a music geek's choice). They care about how things look and feel – and Apple's brilliant look and feel have won it not only legions of loyal customers, but legions of loyal customers who will pay a significant premium. These are typified by the stereotype of the Apple 'fanboi', a slavish devotee of the company and its products, who is best summed by a faux interview on the satirical site the *Onion*, in which a fanboi says 'I'll buy almost anything if it's shiny and made by Apple.'

However, despite a long run of successes, there are a few storm clouds in Jobs's universe. iPod sales have levelled off, and Android phones (which use Google's free open-source operating system) are making serious inroads into a market that the iPhone, until recently, ruled unchallenged. Indeed, for tech observers, it's interesting to watch the Microsoft–Google–Apple dynamic change. A few years back, both Google and Apple were anti-Microsoft. But now things aren't so clear.

By far the biggest worry for Apple (from its fanbois to its staff to shareholders), though, is Jobs's health. He's had serious problems over the last 10 years – first with pancreatic cancer and then with a liver transplant. So the big question that is being asked is: what happens to Apple if Jobs leaves? The precedent from the mid-1990s is not good. It is often said that in Apple only one person's opinion counts – that of Steve Jobs. Can the company continue to be Apple without him?

References and further reading

Aguilar, Quinn (2010) Do you know Steve Jobs?, *Silicon Valley Curious*, 20 June
Apple website, www.apple.com

Appleyard, Bryan (2009) Steve Jobs: the man who polished Apple, *Times*, 16 August

Booth, Cathy, Jackson, David S and Marchant, Valerie (1997) Steve's job: restart Apple, *Time*, 18 August

Campbell, Duncan (2004) Profile: Steve Jobs, *Guardian*, 18 June

Cnet.com, Apple turns 30

Elkind, Peter (2008) The trouble with Steve Jobs, *Fortune*, 5 March

Lohr, Steve (1997) Creating jobs, *New York Times Magazine*, 12 January

Markides, Constantinos C and Geroski, Paul A (2004) *Fast Second: How smart companies bypass radical innovation to enter and dominate new markets*, Jossey-Bass, San Francisco, CA

Usborne, David (2004) The iPod carrier, *Independent on Sunday*, 4 January

Waters, Richard and Menn, Joseph (2010) Silicon Valley visionary who put Apple on top, *Financial Times*, 22 December

Chapter Two
Richard Branson

With over 360 different companies in the Virgin group, interests ranging from mobile phones and internet to trains and drinks, and a net worth of £2.6 billion, Richard Branson is probably the UK's best-known entrepreneur. Much of this is down to his all-conquering love of publicity; sometimes it's difficult to tell whether he's a businessman or a celebrity. But whatever the case, the famously bearded British businessman has been in the headlines for the last 30 years. In 1986, the *Sunday Times* wrote, 'Whether advertising cars or credit cards, sitting in the bath playing with a model aircraft, or setting out to conquer the Atlantic... Branson nowadays sells himself as assiduously and imaginatively as his innumerable companies sell their records, films, et al' (Brown, 1986).

Little has changed in the intervening quarter of a century. At 60, Branson is still ubiquitous and is still very much the face of the Virgin brand. The only real difference is that he has rather more competition these days. When he first noticed that celebrity could work for a business as well as it worked for pop stars and artists, most UK businesspeople were buttoned up and reserved, and the idea of using stunts and themselves to sell their products would have seemed not so much unseemly as simply unimaginable. Now, in many cases, businesspeople are household names, and Branson has gone from being a maverick to a trailblazer.

Branson was born in 1950 near Guildford in Surrey. His father was a lawyer, something of a family tradition, while his mother had been a dancer and an air hostess in South America. He did not excel at school – the reason for this, he would later discover, was that he was dyslexic – but he was a good athlete and, with the help of a crammer, got into Stowe, a famous independent school. He showed early form as an entrepreneur when, at the age of 16, he launched a magazine called *Student* while still at school (previous failed business ventures included attempts at breeding budgies and growing Christmas trees). He ran the magazine for the next three years, and his circulation reached 100,000.

In 1969, Branson ran an ad in his magazine for discounted mail order records. The record industry at the time was something of a closed shop where labels and shops conspired to keep profits fat, and the response to Branson's ad was huge. The only trouble was that he had no stock, but eventually he found a shop that would sell to him. Records, he decided, were far more profitable than magazines, and he closed *Student*. This was the start of his mail order music operation. The Virgin name, incidentally, is supposed to have come from an employee, the thinking being that they were all new to business – it is not as popularly supposed anything to do with the Virgin Islands.

Meanwhile, Branson's girlfriend was pregnant, and the duo struggled to find help and advice. The baby was aborted, but shocked by the lack of support Branson set up the Student Advisory Centre to help young people with problems such as unwanted pregnancy and trouble with drugs. All these activities gave him quite a public profile, and by the time he was 20 in 1971 he'd already made a considerable splash and was the subject of a BBC documentary, which featured, among other things, a slightly surreal sequence of him walking along a river, chewing a hayseed and talking about the difficulty they had getting an abortion. But as much as that, it was about his business ventures and a young man going places.

Virgin's early years were pretty hand-to-mouth. The company had been hit by a huge tax bill, and staff would sometimes pretend no one was in when debt collectors knocked on the door. In late 1970 – largely because of a postal strike – Branson decided that he needed physical premises, and he found a space above a shoe shop on Tottenham Court Road; he opened his first record shop in January 1971. His philosophy remained the same – big volumes and big discounts – and he expanded rapidly, mainly because he thought the competition would try to crush him if he didn't. Around this time, he was memorably described as 'a public school Arthur Daley'.

Having incurred the displeasure of the big labels, he also had his eye on creating a label of his own. Now with significant cash, he bought a manor house near Oxford and turned it into a recording studio; in 1972, he founded the Virgin record label. The company's first signing – Mike Oldfield – recorded *Tubular Bells*, which went on to sell 5 million copies. After a brief dip in its fortunes, the label signed the Sex Pistols in 1977. At the time they were so controversial that no other label would touch them. It was a bold move and one that paid huge dividends in terms of publicity. Throughout the late 1970s and 1980s Branson continued to expand, revelling in his new-found role as the UK's favourite entrepreneur. Moreover, as his empire grew, those who had dismissed him as a 'hippy capitalist' found they were having to take him rather more seriously.

In 1984, Virgin launched the Virgin Atlantic airline, which is now the UK's second-largest long-haul airline. The following year Branson attempted to win the Blue Riband by setting a new record for crossing the Atlantic. The boat, the *Virgin Atlantic Challenger*, sank, but the publicity did Branson no harm. The following year he broke the record in the *Virgin Atlantic Challenger II*. The rest of the 1980s were a whirl of ventures. Virgin Records went international. Virgin launched an airship and balloon company, started a condom brand, went into hotels, and entered – and exited – satellite broadcasting. The group's one big stumble in the 1980s was its 1986 flotation. This lasted all of two years (but managed to take in Black Monday). In 1988, Branson took the group back into private hands. He was, he said, sick of the City's suits and its short-termist approach – and, it be must said, many in the City said they were sick of Branson.

The 1990s saw much of the same: books, vodka and cola, radio, bridal services, trains, cosmetics, gyms and mobiles all caught Branson's attention. In 1992, he had to sell Virgin Music to EMI to bail out his airline; he said he cried when the deal went through, as Virgin Music was his first business. He also tried to win operation of the UK's National Lottery, promising all his proceeds would go to charity – but he lost to the Camelot consortium. Meanwhile his record-breaking – and publicity-gathering – attempts continued apace, moving from the sea to the air. In 1991, he crossed the Pacific in a balloon, breaking a record. And, from 1995 to 1998, he attempted several circumnavigations of the world in a balloon; his team were beaten to the prize by the *Breitling Orbiter 3* in 1999. By way of consolation he became Sir Richard Branson in the millennium New Year honours list.

The 2000s were scarcely any quieter and, although by this stage Branson was in his 50s, the trademark blond mane and beard were still there. Virgin launched Virgin Blue, a low-cost Australian airline; Branson sold the British and Irish Virgin Megastores; he launched Virgin Fuel, a company to produce clean fuel, in keeping with his increasing interest in solving environmental issues… and the rather breathless list goes on and on. A few ventures do stick out though. First, Virgin Money, his financial services group, came very close to buying the troubled UK bank Northern Rock; ultimately it didn't, and the Rock remained a ward of the UK state. His second headline-grabbing venture was Virgin Galactic, which is devoted to space travel for tourists; the company is currently taking bookings and is entirely serious about the undertaking. Finally, in 2007, with Al Gore, he launched the Virgin Earth Challenge Prize to combat global warming – the prize goes to the first person or group to come up with a means of scrubbing a billion tons of CO_2 out of the atmosphere every year for 10 years.

What Branson has consistently done best is personify the Virgin brand. Of course, there are plenty of other people who embody their brands – Steve Jobs, Warren Buffett and the late Anita Roddick spring to mind – but Branson is different because in all of these cases there is a kind of core product, whether it's personal electronics or investments or cosmetics. With Branson, the product is secondary. The Virgin brand can be slapped on anything, whether it's condoms or vodka or mobiles or planes. Sometimes it works; sometimes it doesn't. But you've got to give it a go, and when things don't work out people rarely hold it against Branson.

Even the publicity stunts – which might look ridiculous on someone less comfortable with his own celebrity – add to the brand, because they're entirely consistent with who Branson is. You could probably make a case that Branson's entire life sometimes seems to be a publicity stunt – but that doesn't really diminish him. It's probably because he seems to be having so much fun whatever it is that he's doing. The BBC journalist Robert Peston (2009) referred to something called the 'The entrepreneur's wound', that is, the unpleasant childhood or traumatic experience that drives many people to succeed but means they are never satisfied and never happy. Branson is quite the opposite. He's hyperactive and driven, certainly, but he seems to do it because he genuinely enjoys it.

For all Branson's love of publicity, though, there is one area where this notoriously public figure is a notoriously private one. Those who look into Branson's financial affairs usually come out little the wiser. The book *Branson* by the celebrated investigative journalist Tom Bower paints a picture of a man who often sails very close to the wind, and whose group has often been faced with the very real prospect of insolvency. A question many ask is: which of Branson's companies actually make money (and which of them are subsidized by those that do)? In fact, Virgin's holding company's accounts have often shown little real money being made outside the airlines. It is for this reason, so the thinking goes, that Branson likes his companies private, not because City suits are stodgy and unimaginative. Bower paints Branson as a shameless self-publicist, a sharp operator and a man whose greatest talent is separating bankers from their money.

Branson's endless stunts may also have started to pall. In 2008, the *Economist* noted that these days Branson spends precious little time in the country of his birth: 'The British took Sir Richard to their hearts originally for his rebellious image, but many have grown weary of his self-publicising. Maybe Americans will applaud his chutzpah.' There may be some truth in all of this, but it's a little early to consign Branson to history. He turned 60 in 2010 (but looks 15 years younger); it seems very unlikely that he is going to grow old gracefully.

References and further reading

Appleyard, Bryan (1986) Record maker with no flip side, *Times*, 30 October

Blackhurst, Chris (1998) At the court of King Richard, *Management Today*, 1 April

Bower, Tom (2000) *Branson*, Fourth Estate, London

Branson, Richard (1998) *Losing My Virginity*

Branson, Richard (2009) *Business Stripped Bare: Adventures of a Global Entrepreneur*

Brown, Mick (1986) Profile of Richard Branson, *Sunday Times*, 8 June

Moore, Martha T (1995) Rash, brash Branson has Virgin soaring, *USA Today*, 5 July

New Zealand Herald (2008) Branson: walking on water, or on thin ice, 3 October

Peston, Robert (2009) *The Entrepreneur's Wound*, BBC Radio 4, 30 October

Specter, Michael (2007) A modern knight, *Australian Women's Weekly*, 31 August

Chapter Three
Warren Buffett

Most company annual general meetings are dull affairs, where the only excitement is provided by activist shareholders kicking up a fuss (although they have virtually no voting power, compared to institutional shareholders who usually don't even bother showing up). At Berkshire Hathaway, it's rather different. Attendance is around the 30,000 mark despite the event being held in the decidedly backwater town of Omaha, Nebraska. Berkshire Hathaway's AGM is the second-biggest annual event in the town after the College World Series Baseball Tournament.

Much of this, says Kelly Broz, the company's Annual Meeting Director, is down to the business's legendary founder: 'Shareholders are interested in what Warren and [co-founder] Charlie [Munger] have to say about not only Berkshire operations but their business philosophies and views on the economy in general. Also, Warren and Charlie are incredibly funny together. It's not only educational but entertaining to hear them on stage during the six-hour Q&A session.'

Warren Buffett is an extraordinary figure. He looks not so much like a billionaire as an ordinary guy or perhaps a college lecturer. He lives modestly. He is immensely pithy and quotable: gems such as 'It's only when the tide goes out that you realize who's been swimming naked' seem to trip off his tongue. He's also extraordinarily modest and self-deprecating and has ascribed much of his fortune to luck: 'If you stick me down in the middle of Bangladesh or Peru or someplace, you find out how much this talent is going to produce in the wrong kind of soil.' And most importantly he is the world's most successful investor. It is no great stretch to say that, were it not for Buffett, many people would not have heard of Nebraska.

Like many great investment strategies, Buffett's is extraordinarily simple. He only invests in companies he understands, whose management he believes in, and that he thinks have good prospects for long-term growth. He buys shares and companies that he believes are worth holding on to. This simple strategy has made Buffett the third-richest man in the world – although it's worth noting that he has also been the richest and the second richest. He's well known as a contrarian – Buffett is often seen heading in the opposite direction to people who are making huge amounts of money by following conventional wisdom. He famously sat out the dotcom boom and eschewed derivatives in the 2000s. But, as these two examples show, although Buffett is sometimes wrong in the short term, he's usually proved right in the medium to long term. For these reasons he is often called either 'the Sage of Omaha' or 'the Oracle of Omaha'.

Buffett was born in 1930, the son of a Republican congressman and stockbroker. Like many ultra-successful businesspeople, he showed aptitude at an early age. Aged six, he was splitting Coca-Cola six-packs and reselling them at a 20 per cent profit. At 11, he famously bought his first shares for $38 each. They promptly fell to $27, but recovered to $40, when he sold them. Although he made a small profit, had he held on longer he'd have done better, as the shares later reached $200; this is often cited as an early lesson in long-termism. He filed his first income tax form in 1944. Before he'd graduated from high school he'd hired out pinball machines, saved thousands from paper rounds (tens of thousands in today's money), and bought 40 acres of farmland, which he rented out to a tenant farmer.

After graduation he didn't want to go to college, but his father prevailed and he went to Wharton business school at the University of Pennsylvania, before transferring to the University of Nebraska. There he read Benjamin Graham's book *The Intelligent Investor*, which advised investors to seek out what the author called cigar-butt companies – undervalued businesses with a few puffs of life in them. After graduating, Buffett was famously rejected by Harvard Business School and went to study at Columbia. With a Master's in economics under his belt, he went to work for Graham.

Buffett was starting to develop investment ideas of his own: rather than find dying companies he could squeeze a little value out of, he was becoming more interested in buying well-managed but unfashionable businesses. In 1957, he set up an investment partnership in Nebraska. He aimed to beat the Dow by 10 per cent; when the partnership was dissolved 12 years later, he'd managed a rate of just under 30 per cent, while the Dow had appreciated by 7.4 per cent.

But it was in 1962 that the foundations for the institution we know today were laid. In 1962, he bought a troubled Massachusetts-based textile company called Berkshire Hathaway; it was, as Graham would have it, a cigar butt. However, Buffett didn't just want to squeeze the last few drops of value out of it, so he started redirecting its resources into other areas, most notably insurance. This gave him a regular income stream of cheap capital – and more importantly the gap between receiving the payments and settling the claims meant that Buffett had a large pool of cash. Best of all, this was at a time when the stock markets were depressed. It was a perfect combination of circumstances for a man who specialized in seeing long-term value where others couldn't.

And this, essentially, has been the Buffett strategy. The company's annual report and accounts have a nice comparison with its performance against that of the S&P 500. Between 1965 and 2009 (the last report available) Berkshire Hathaway has averaged 20.3 per cent a year, compounded; the S&P 500 has gained 9.3 per cent.

In rather blunter terms, $100 invested in the S&P in 1965 would be worth $5,430; invested in Berkshire Hathaway it would be worth $434,057. Indeed, Berkshire Hathaway has created a fair few 'surprise' millionaires in Omaha.

Buffett has not always been lauded, however. He famously sat out the dotcom boom – as the bubbling tech stocks were neither long-term holds nor something he understood. In 1999, Berkshire Hathaway shares made 0.5 per cent, while the S&P managed 21 per cent and the NASDAQ index grew by over 80 per cent. And, as the NASDAQ reached dizzying heights and a lot of people drank the Kool-Aid and really started to believe that share prices had somehow become permanently decoupled from things like the ability to make money, Buffett came in for a lot of criticism. Then, on 10 March 2000, the bubble burst, and in the following three years Berkshire Hathaway managed overall gains (it lost money in 2001), while the S&P did nothing but fall. As for the NASDAQ, over 10 years later, it still hasn't recovered and is something like 50 per cent of its dotcom peak. In the space of a year, Buffett went from being a dinosaur who didn't get the new economy to one of the few people clever enough to invest only in what he understood. Another brick was laid in the temple of Buffett the investment guru.

The pattern was to repeat itself nearly a decade later. With his usual mixture of prescience and folksiness, Buffett was warning about the dangers of the ballooning trade in exotic financial instruments not long after the dotcom crash. In Berkshire Hathaway's 2002 annual report he wrote, 'I view derivatives as time bombs, both for the parties that deal in them and the economic system', said they were 'financial weapons of mass destruction' and also likened them to 'hell… easy to enter and almost impossible to exit'. This, as it turned out, was absolutely on the money and in characteristic Buffett style, in language anyone could understand. Of course, he was right. And, while 2008 was Berkshire's worst year ever, it lost a mere 9.6 per cent, compared to the S&P's 37 per cent.

Moreover, in the very bleakest days of 2008 when most of the financial world was wondering where everything was going, Buffett was going shopping. Towards the end of the year, he picked up a $5 billion chunk of Goldman Sachs, following another of his nostrums, 'Be fearful when others are greedy; be greedy when others are fearful.' And, in the first half of 2010, when knives were really out for the bank, Buffett offered a ringing endorsement of its embattled CEO, Lloyd Blankfein.

So is there anything bad to say about him? Well, he has made blunders – but in many cases, such as US Airways in the 1990s, a willingness to hold on for years has often meant that eventually the stocks have bounced back. The cult of Buffett, the devotional literature he inspires and his rather glassy-eyed followers can grate a bit. But it's difficult to find much to dislike about this admirably honest and modest man. He practises exactly what he preaches. He pays himself a salary of $100,000 a year, which is a pittance in a country where far less successful CEOs routinely pay themselves millions. He dines on burgers and drinks Coke, drives an old car and lives in a house in Omaha that he bought in 1957 for $31,500, although he does have a beach house in Laguna Beach worth around $4 million. In 1989 he bought a private jet, which he named the *Indefensible* as a humorous jibe at himself, as he'd previously been highly critical of CEO excess in areas like transportation.

Still, the image of a man unaffected by wealth despite having been the world's wealthiest is largely true. People who send him unsolicited business ideas often get considered, thoughtful replies, there are endless stories about how he never pulls the 'Do you know who I am card?', and journalists who call his PA to get an interview sometimes find themselves speaking to Buffett himself, as he often answers his own phone.

As Buffett is now in his 80s he has said he is looking for a successor, and the rumours are that it could be Ajit Jain, the head of Berkshire's reinsurance operations, whom Buffett has described as a 'superstar'.

It is entirely in keeping with Buffett's philosophy – and his outspoken disdain for inherited wealth – that his children will inherit very little of his fortune. He has stated on numerous occasions that those who grow up with great wealth are members of the 'lucky sperm club' and has said, 'I want to give my kids just enough so that they would feel that they could do anything, but not so much that they would feel like doing nothing.' As for his vast fortune, he announced in 2006 that he would give 85 per cent of his Berkshire Hathaway holdings to charity and that five-sixths of it would go to the Bill & Melinda Gates Foundation, which focuses on healthcare, poverty and education (Buffett and the Gateses are good friends). The value of the gift was reckoned to be about $37 billion in 2006, the largest act of philanthropy ever. He further indicated that the remaining 15 per cent would also go to charity.

In 2010, he and Bill Gates proposed that the wealthy should commit at least half their fortunes to charity. In a letter to *Fortune* magazine, Buffett wrote:

> My luck was accentuated by my living in a market system that sometimes produces distorted results, though overall it serves our country well... I've worked in an economy that rewards someone who saves the lives of others on a battlefield with a medal, rewards a great teacher with thank-you notes from parents, but rewards those who can detect the mispricing of securities with sums reaching into the billions. In short, fate's distribution of long straws is wildly capricious.

Giving the vast bulk of his fortune away, he believes, is the best way of compensating for all the good fortune he has enjoyed.

References and further reading

Berkshire Hathaway company reports and accounts
Berkshire Hathaway website, www.berkshirehathaway.com
Cornwell, Rupert (2002) Profile, *Independent on Sunday*, 27 July
Kanter, Larry (1999) Warren Buffet, *Salon.com*, 31 August
Loomis, Carol J (2006) Warren Buffett gives away his fortune, *Fortune*, 25 June

Rigby, Rhymer (2004) Naked ambition and how to get it, *Management Today*, 1 September

Rigby, Rhymer (2009) AGMs that rally investors with a share of the fun, *Financial Times*, 10 February

Schroeder, Alice (2008) *The Snowball: Warren Buffett and the business of life*, Random House, New York

Sullivan, Aline (1997) Buffett, the Sage of Omaha, makes value strategy seem simple: secrets of a High Plains investor, *New York Times*, 20 December

Chapter Four
Jeff Bezos

If Andy Grove personifies Silicon Valley Mark I, and Steve Jobs Silicon Valley Mark II, then Jeff Bezos is the living, breathing avatar of Silicon Valley Mark III – the dotcom revolution. The company he still heads up, Amazon, was launched in 1995 as a Seattle-based online bookseller. In its early years, in true dotcom style, the business burnt its way through over half a billion dollars. But unlike so many other dotcoms, it survived to become a global giant that is now worth $56 billion: it not only survived but thrived and became a colossal part of the retail landscape.

But although Bezos and Amazon are often used as shorthand for everything dotcom, the fact that they survived while so many others failed is because, in many important respects, they were not typical dotcoms at all. For starters, the company's focus was always squarely on customers and giving them the best possible experience; this is something Bezos maintains a messianic zeal about. Secondly, unlike the case in many dotcoms, Bezos was very upfront about how the company was going to make no money for four or five years. And thirdly the company stuck to its guns right through the dotcom crash when others were losing their heads.

Bezos was born in Albuquerque, New Mexico in 1964. His mother was still a teenager when she had him, and her marriage to his father was a very short-lived one; she remarried when he was four. His maternal grandfather, who owned a large ranch, was a regional director of the Atomic Energy Commission and was a significant influence on the young Jeffrey. As a child, Bezos was notable for one thing: he was very, very clever, with a particular aptitude for science, and from an early age displayed great inventiveness. His early precociousness was a sign of things to come: he went on to win science prizes and study at Princeton University. There, he started reading physics but changed to computers and eventually took a degree in computer science and electrical engineering.

After graduating in 1986, Bezos went to work in finance. He was employed at several Wall Street firms, where computer science was finding fashion as a tool for predicting stock market trends. In 1994 he was working at the hedge fund DE Shaw when he had a kind of eureka moment. This was that the number of internet users was growing at over 2,300 per cent a year. So Bezos, who is famed for being painstaking and methodical, looked at the top 20 mail order businesses to see which would work best in the new medium. He plumped for books, as they were a natural for the mail order market but for one problem – a mail order catalogue for books would be huge, which meant that the nascent internet could offer a significant advance. That said, this was all rather hypothetical. At the time, e-commerce didn't really exist; very few people even had e-mail.

Continuing his diligence, Bezos's next port of call was the American Booksellers' convention in Los Angeles, where he discovered that book wholesalers had electronic lists of their products. His belief that bookselling belonged online grew. His first USP was an obvious one – an online bookstore could offer far greater variety than one that had to physically shelve stock. Moreover, books were a great product to sell online – their weight-to-value ratio means that posting isn't a problem, they aren't perishable, and people are generally prepared to wait a few days for them. Moreover, large numbers of people live a long way from a well-stocked bookstore, especially in the United States; for them an online bookseller would be a godsend.

But Bezos couldn't interest his employers, so he decided to take the plunge, along with his wife. He drew up a business plan and in 1994 founded Amazon.com, with family and friends acting as the first investors. In the best tradition of West Coast start-ups, Amazon's birthplace was a humble one – the garage of a two-bedroom house in Seattle. The city was chosen because of the high concentration of people with computer skills, and it's said that Nick Hanauer, a Seattle businessman and the first 'outside' investor in Amazon, persuaded Bezos to make the move. Hanauer put $40,000 into the fledgling company, convinced of Amazon's advantages; at the height of the dotcom boom his investment was worth $250 million. Once Bezos had tested the site on friends and was convinced the site worked as it should he launched his online bookstore in July 1995. According to the company's website, the first book it sold was *Fluid Concepts and Creative Analogies: Computer models of the fundamental mechanisms of thought.*

Amazon quickly became a dotcom darling. Bezos dealt with the media well, and books were things people actually wanted to buy online. In 1997, the company raised $54 million in its initial public offering, and in October that year the company fulfilled its millionth order – with his eye for publicity Bezos hand-delivered it to Japan. But already the naysayers had their eye on a less impressive metric – how much money the company was losing. Bezos had always said that initially growth was more important than profitability and that he expected to lose money – but the amount he was losing was causing some to question this strategy.

Amazon also began to diversify: in 1998 it opened a music store, and in 1999 it moved into electronics and clothes. It also began to look beyond the United States – in 1998 it moved into Germany and the UK. Traffic boomed: in 1999 the company's sales were a heady $1.6 billion, and by many metrics – sales, presence and that old dotcom rubric eyeballs – the company looked great. Indeed, *Time* magazine made Bezos its person of the year (Ramo, 1999). But by another very important metric things weren't so rosy. By November 1999, total losses were over half a billion dollars, and still Bezos was cautioning against rushing to profitability. This continued right through the next year, when the dotcom bubble burst. In June 2000, the company's stock fell by 19 per cent when a report suggested that it might run out of cash, yet it opened stores in France and Japan. In 2001 came more of the same – Amazon said it would be cutting its workforce, there were more rumours, and there was more speculation that the company was going to be yet another dotcom casualty – wags joked about Amazon.bomb and Amazon.toast. Yet Bezos held his nerve, and the closest he got to truly acknowledging that things might not be going to plan was in his 2001 letter to shareholders where he said 'Ouch. It's been a brutal year.' Indeed it had: Amazon had lost $1.4 billion.

I remember interviewing Jeff Bezos around this time. Journalistically, it wasn't my finest hour. It was a ridiculously hot day – one of the hottest ever in London – and I decided that it would be cool to do the interview in a pair of shorts, as this was still the dressed-down world of dotcom. I'm not sure what Bezos really thought about this, and he cracked a couple of jokes. It wasn't the greatest of interviews – I was convinced that he was coming out with a load of corporate boilerplate when he should be admitting that Amazon was never going to be profitable. Now, of course, I realize that Bezos was simply saying what he genuinely believed, that the then fashionable nostrum that Amazon was finished was completely wrong and that I was far from the smartest guy in the room. Then again, what do you get from someone who shows up to interview *Time*'s man of the year in a pair of shorts?

But the pressure was now on, and Bezos had to do something, so he said the company would be profitable by the end of the year. In early 2002, the company reported a very, very small profit for the fourth quarter of 2001, beating everyone's expectations. It would report its first annual profit in early 2004 for the year 2003, some seven years after it was founded. This was a rather healthier $125 million. It would seem that Jeff Bezos, the long-term dotcommer, had been right after all. He'd shrugged off the doubters and the snipers, weathered the bust and built the biggest online retailer of them all. These days, the only US retailer that exceeds Amazon in terms of market capitalization is Walmart. In the UK in 2009 it was voted the nation's third favourite retailer (by Verdict Research) after John Lewis and IKEA.

Since proving to be a viable business, Amazon has continued to move on and innovate. It bought the Chinese site Joyo.com in 2004 and renamed it Amazon.cn in 2007; and it has expanded into every category imaginable. In the early 2000s, it began selling other people's products as well as its own and as a result has become a vast online marketplace with thousands of sellers rather than just a retailer. In 2007, the company started selling MP3 downloads, putting it in direct competition with Apple's all-conquering iTunes. But again it did it differently – whereas iTunes and others sold music with DRM (digital rights management, meaning that you couldn't copy it), Amazon's was DRM free – and MP3, a format that will play on virtually any device. This was a key differentiator and immediately endeared Amazon to many consumers who had struggled with Apple's perceived control-freakery. Amazon now has 12 per cent of the market against Apple's 70 per cent (NPD Group, May 2010), but the latter's share is flat while Amazon's is growing. The company's other notable innovation has been the Kindle, an e-book reader. In 2010, it was thought that around 8 million of the dedicated e-book readers had been sold. By way of contrast, in 2010 Apple sold approximately 15 million of its tablet computer, the iPad – a device that can also be used to read books, although unlike the dedicated Kindle not in bright sunlight.

Of course, there have been mistakes along the way. Bezos has said: 'We were investors in every bankrupt, 1999-vintage ecommerce start-up. Pets.com, living.com, kozmo.com. We invested in a lot of high profile flame-outs. The only good thing is we had lots of company. It didn't take us off our own mission but it was a waste of capital' (Quittner, 2008). The company also attempted to go into search (lesson – don't take on Google). But the big difference between Amazon and so many dotbombs is that with Amazon the fundamentals always felt right. There was a clear vision and a sensible plan, Bezos was always a great details man, and company always represented a better way of doing things. Moreover, Amazon has always been fanatical about the customer experience and including its customers in the process. The vast amounts of data it collects not only allow it to refine its offerings to 'shops for a single customer' but they also make the site feel like a community where people's opinions about their purchases really matter and help others.

At the *Wired* 'Disruptive by design' conference in 2009, in a Q&A with Steve Levy, Bezos was asked what had allowed Amazon to survive where so many had doubted him. He replied:

> There were two things: the business metrics, and the stock price. After the bust, the stock price went down, but the business metrics continued to improve... We had some very harsh critics during that time, but we always noticed that our harshest critics were among our best customers. Having a team that is heads down focused on building product makes you more resilient against outside opinion.

It's worth remembering too that much as Bezos was a voice of optimism in the bust he was also a voice of sober restraint during the worst excesses of the boom. A mantra he often repeated to staff was 'Don't feel 30 per cent smarter because the stock is up 30 per cent this month, because you'll have to feel 30 per cent dumber when it goes down.' He also said, 'One of the differences between founder/entrepreneurs and financial managers is that founder/entrepreneurs are stubborn about the vision of the business, and keep working the details. The trick to being an entrepreneur is to know when to be stubborn and when to be flexible. The trick for me is to be stubborn about the big things.'

Yet Bezos is not an entrepreneur in the mould of Branson. He has said on a number of occasions that he has no particular desire to run off and found another company. He does, however, have other interests – and one of these is about space travel, which arguably is the ultimate rich man's hobby these days. In 2005, Bezos announced Blue Origin, which is a project to put paying passengers into space. His sale in 2010 of 2 million Amazon shares (leaving him with a mere 92 million) led to speculation that he might be speeding up activities in this sphere. Even if it is just a hobby, with Bezos behind it we should certainly watch this space.

References and further reading

Achievement.org, Biography of Jeff Bezos

Anderson, Chris (2001) The zen of Jeff Bezos, *Wired*, 13

Businessweek (2006) Jeff Bezos' risky bet, 13 November

Deutschman, Alan (2004) Inside the mind of Jeff Bezos, *Fast Company*, 1 August

Frey, Christine and Cokk, John (2004) How amazon.com survived, thrived and turned a profit, *Seattle Post-Intelligencer*, 28 January

Quittner, Josh (2008) The charmed life of Amazon's Jeff Bezos, *Fortune*, 15 April

Ramo, Joshua Cooper (1999) Jeffrey Preston Bezos, person of the year, *Time*, 27 December

Rigby, Rhymer (2001) Interview with Jeff Bezos, *Business 2.0*

Chapter Five
The Google Duo
(Sergey Brin and
Larry Page)

Thanks in part to a *Playboy* article published in September 2004, Sergey Brin and Larry Page will forever be known as the 'Google guys' ('The Google guys – America's newest billionaires'). And although this alliterative cuteness may seem a rather trivial way to describe two of the world's richest and most influential technology entrepreneurs, this is exactly what they are. Playboy's headline merely gave us a convenient shorthand for it. Brin and Page are co-founders of the world's biggest search engine, one of its hottest tech companies and, according to some, its most valuable brand. The duo are currently Technology President (Brin) and CEO (Page) and have significant shareholdings in the company; Eric Schmidt, whom they recruited in 2001, was CEO until early 2011.

Page was born in Michigan and studied there before enrolling as a PhD student at Stanford in California. Brin was born in Russia, and his parents emigrated to the United States in 1979; he graduated from the University of Maryland before moving to Stanford to do a doctorate in computer science. The two became friends and then, in 1996, began working together on a search engine that was then called Backrub. In 1997, they decided to change the name to Google, a play on the mathematical term 'googol' (one followed by 100 zeros) and an allusion to the already vast amount of online information.

In true Silicon Valley style, the pair managed to convince Sun co-founder Andy Bechtolsheim to invest $100,000. They set up shop in a rented garage and incorporated as Google Technology Inc. The domain google.com was registered in September 1997, and the company was incorporated a year later. Soon, they'd hired their first employee, Craig Silverstein, who is still Director of Technology. In a 2008 interview with *The Times* (London), Mr Silverstein said, 'I always imagined we were going to be an 80 to 100-person company.' The company now has over 20,000 employees. By the end of its first year, PC World had crowned it the top search engine. This was the beginning of what was going to be a remarkable ascent – from a company few had heard of to a globe-spanning colossus in under a decade.

So what did the Google duo do that was so different? They certainly weren't the first. In fact, if you look back at the list of search engines (Excite, Ask Jeeves, Lycos – all of which are now pale shadows of their former selves), Google was a very late entrant, but what it offered users was different in certain ways. First, it ranked pages differently. Other search engines mainly ranked on the number of times the search term appeared on the page in question; Google recognized that important pages were likely to be linked to by other pages, and its PageRank algorithm analysed this. The results, it was said, were more akin to the way an individual would assign importance to a page. Page said in a 2001 interview with *Businessweek* that: 'We realized by talking to all the CEOs of search companies – which were really turning into portals – that commercially, no one was going to develop search engines. They said, "Oh, we don't really care about our search engine." And we realized there was a huge business opportunity and that nobody else was going to work on it.'

Google's second big differentiator was how clean its page looked. In an era when many search engines and portals took a kitchen-sink approach to their front pages, Google's was an exercise in minimalism. It was – as it's always been – essentially a search box, the word 'Google' and a white background. All of this endeared it to users, but it didn't bring in revenues.

Google's differences from more run-of-the-mill dotcoms didn't stop with user experience and technology either. Its third big difference appeared in 2000 when Google started selling ads based on users' searches. These are the ads that usually appear down the right side of the page, and the revenue model was (and is) a combination of companies 'buying' these keywords in an auction process and click-throughs, that is, the company pays Google a sum when users click through from Google to the company's site. This meant that, unlike so many dotcom start-ups, Google had a decent revenue stream from very early days. It didn't have to spend years burning investors' cash coming up with ever more elaborate reasons why visitor numbers were more important than profitability. Instead, the company first turned a profit in late 2001, about three years after it was incorporated.

The company's final great difference is cultural. It has long been famed as a great place to work – and is legendary for everything from the quality of its cafeteria food, to child care, to having fun facilities like climbing walls for staff. When I wrote a weekly slot for the *Financial Times* on the quirky and enjoyable side of corporate life, I had a self-imposed rule that I could only use Google once every three months – as, whatever it was, they always seemed to have it. You certainly get the impression that this culture emanates from the very top. When I interviewed Sergey Brin in 2001, he seemed very much a regular guy, albeit one who was uncommonly clever. His office was a bit of a mess, and the corner was full of skiing equipment; we spent 15 minutes of the interview talking about skiing at Lake Tahoe.

Perhaps the most famous manifestation of the Google philosophy is the informal motto, 'Don't be evil'. Page, Brin and Schmidt famously explained this in an 'owners' manual' prior to the company's 2004 initial public offering (IPO); it may have been partly to assuage staff worries that being listed would change the culture: 'Don't be evil.

We believe strongly that in the long term, we will be better served – as shareholders and in all other ways – by a company that does good things for the world even if we forgo some short term gains. This is an important aspect of our culture and is broadly shared within the company.' The company later revised this to an 'evil scale', which it publishes on its website under corporate information.

The company's IPO raised $1.67 billion and made many employees millionaires – but, although the company is listed, Page and Brin retained a majority shareholding, giving them ultimate control. And after its successful IPO it certainly didn't rest on its laurels or remain 'just' a search business.

Its highly profitable core (it controls over two-thirds of the online advertising market) has allowed it to pursue a very unusual game plan. Essentially, it has spent much of the last seven or eight years coming up with brilliant, innovative and usually well-designed products and then giving them away free.

The best known of these is Gmail, its e-mail service – this has proved so popular and been so well received (largely because of the quality of its design, which revolutionized webmail) that some companies such as Rentokil have switched their corporate systems over to it (*IT Pro*, 13 October 2009). Again Google was a late entrant to the market. Its main competitors are Hotmail, which has been around since 1996 and was bought by Microsoft in 1997, and Yahoo Mail, which debuted in 1997. Gmail didn't appear until 2004. Nonetheless it has made impressive inroads into the market. Hotmail has 360 million users, Yahoo 284 million and Gmail 173 million.

It should also be noted that Gmail is widely seen as cooler and more cutting-edge than either of its rivals. Indeed, Hotmail was recently given a makeover – and, according to the *New York Times* Tech blog (18 May 2010), the reason for doing so was to make it more like Gmail. Hotmail suffers in the United States from a bit of a 'perception problem', as the Microsoft vice president Chris Jones put it. People perceive that Hotmail is plagued by spam, has low storage, is missing a lot of features and is basically yesteryear's e-mail service. 'This is partially because Hotmail has been around for a while', Jones said, celebrating Hotmail as the first web e-mail service to hit it really big. 'Of late, Gmail has been first with a big inbox, the first with IMAP and because of those firsts, it has good buzz going with it.' The last sentence probably tells you almost everything you need to know about the difference between Microsoft and Google.

Gmail may be one of Google's best offerings, but its newer products are equally interesting and even more worrying for competitors. Last year, the company launched its Chrome browser, which was very well received and now has just under 7 per cent of the market, behind Firefox with around 25 per cent and Internet Explorer with 60 per cent (Netmarketshare, 2010). Notably, it is ahead of Safari, Apple's proprietary browser. But Chrome points to something even more revolutionary. Google wants not only to provide you with search and mail, but to give you a free operating system too. This puts its tanks squarely on Microsoft's lawn, as the Windows operating system currently runs on over 90 per cent of the world's computers. The point is that Chrome isn't meant to be just a browser – one of its future permutations will be as an operating system. Based on Linux, it will be open-source (meaning anyone can view and alter the code) and free. It's designed to be lightweight and should work best on smaller laptops where, the idea is, it will provide a near 'instant on'. Of course, there have been free Linux-based operating systems around for years. But none of them has come anywhere near mainstream adoption on desktops and laptops; the biggest, Ubuntu, is reckoned to have about 12 million users. Part of this has been because it has insufficient corporate muscle behind it, but a free operating system backed by Google is a very different prospect.

Google already has form in this area – although in this case it has hurt Apple far more than Microsoft. It launched a mobile phone operating system called Android in 2008. Again, this is based on Linux, and the company released it as open-source. Android has been a huge success and, depending on whom you believe, may be either snapping at iPhone's heels or likely to pass it. Certainly, in 2010, some commentators suggested that, when it came to phone features, Apple was now chasing Google rather than the other way around. And as for Microsoft in the phone space? Well, as tech blogger John Gruber put it, 'The big loser this week... was Microsoft. They're simply not even part of the game... They've got nothing. No interesting devices, weak sales, and a shrinking user base. Microsoft's irrelevance is taken for granted.'

The company is unsettling tech's biggest players in other ways too. Google moved very early (2006) into the online applications arena. Online applications are pared-down versions of programs like Word that require nothing more than a computer browser to run – effectively Google is providing a rudimentary version of Office online. It's worth stressing here that Google Apps, even in its paid-for enterprise form, does not match the functionality of MS Office, but it's also worth noting that the vast majority of Office users do not need very much of that functionality – and that in mid-2009 Microsoft launched a free online version of Office.

In fact, when it comes to a lot of its products, Google seems to have it both ways. If it launches first, it is brilliant and innovative, and if it launches late it makes the incumbent look stodgy and unresponsive to users' needs. Many put this down to the corporate culture. Google is widely regarded as having a workforce who are passionate about what they do and a corporate ethos that encourages innovation. The company famously offers its engineers 20 per cent of their time to spend looking at projects they're interested in. Much of this stems from having founders who have such a strong belief in the creative application of new technologies.

Of course, not everything Google touches turns to gold. Google Video Player died a quiet death in 2007 (the company bought YouTube); there's also been Google Orkut, the company's less-than-stellar stab at social networking, and Google Answers, which is nowhere near as successful as its Yahoo counterpart. But when you rank these against Gmail, Google Earth, Google Maps, Google Apps, Chrome and so on, the misses seem a small price to pay. You might argue, though, that Google acts as a disincentive to other innovative companies, as whatever you develop online at some point Google will come along and do a better job; the best you can hope for is to be bought.

Google's enormous success has seen increased scrutiny of its activities by competition watchdogs and complaints about its behaviour and power from competitors. It has also faced increasing concern from privacy advocates who fear that the amount of information the company knows about individuals is staggering. It has gone some way to placate those who fear for their privacy. But the worry always remains – what if the comparatively benign giant decides one day to start using some of the data it holds more aggressively and less scrupulously?

Interestingly, the company's biggest headache to date has been not so much technological as political. Again it's rooted largely in Brin and Page's long-held wish to run a company that does no evil – and the fact that cute mottoes are comparatively easy to live up to when you're the underdog that everyone likes, but less so when you're a market-leading multinational. After much hand-wringing, the company entered China in 2006 with a censored version of its search engine. At the time Brin said, 'We felt perhaps we could compromise our principles but provide ultimately more information for the Chinese [people]... and make a difference.' The company was widely seen as being something of an ethical contortionist here, having betrayed its roots, and it must have been especially hard for Brin, with his memories of growing up in Russia. In the end, combining the Chinese government's desire to control information with Google's wish for it to be free proved an accommodation too far. In March 2010, after hacking attacks that were traced to mainland China, Google announced that it was no longer willing to censor its Chinese search results and Google's Chinese searches would redirect to more liberal Hong Kong. This effectively ended the company's presence in China – although China was one of the few markets where Google wasn't number one.

As for Page and Brin, neither of them is yet 40. According to Forbes, in 2010, together they were the 24th-richest person in the world, and they still hold a substantial chunk of the company's shares and voting power, although they have said they will be selling off chunks to dilute their stake to below 50 per cent. There seems little reason for either to leave a company that at just over 10 years old looks set to continue its record of market-disrupting innovation. That said, both have expressed an interest in renewable energy.

References and further reading

Economist (2008) Enlightenment man, 6 December
Ignatius, Adi (2006) Meet the Google guys, *Time*, 12 February
Kang, Cecilia (2010) Cars and wind: what's next for Google as it pushes beyond the web?, *Washington Post*, 12 October
Malseed, Mark (2007) The story of Sergey Brin, *Moment Magazine*, February
Playboy (2004) Interview: Google guys, September
Rigby, Rhymer (2000) Interview with Sergey Brin, *Business 2.0*
Spiegel (2010) Google co-founder on pulling out of China, 30 March

Chapter Six
Sir Tim Berners-Lee

I t's fair to ask what Tim Berners-Lee – who is not a businessman – is doing on a list of business thinkers. The answer is simple. Berners-Lee is the man who is widely regarded as the father of the world wide web (Al Gore's claims notwithstanding). As a key player in the great technological revolution of the late 20th and early 21st centuries, he's had a far more profound effect on the way we do business – and, for that matter, our lives in general – than hundreds of other people more obviously connected to the world of commerce and industry. Without his work the companies run by some other thinkers in this book such as the Google duo and Jeff Bezos could not exist. Yet unlike them Berners-Lee is not particularly rich and lives the life of an academic, albeit one who has been hailed as the greatest living Briton.

Before we continue, it's important to understand that the web and the internet are not the same thing. The internet is the series of networks (including all the physical computers and wires connected to it). At one end of the scale, this may mean your PC or mobile phone and, at the other, it's Google's vast server farms. The web (or world wide web as Berners-Lee originally called it) is a means of sharing information that is built on top of the net. In terms of the traffic on the net, the web makes up a sizeable chunk of the total, but it's not everything. For instance, e-mail is in the main done over the internet, but not part of the web, unless it's webmail. The internet pre-dates the web by 20 years and has its origins in the US Department of Defense-sponsored Arpanet. The first message was sent over the internet on 29 October 1969, from UCLA to the Stanford Research Institute (the message was the word 'login' although only 'lo' was sent before the system crashed). This date is widely used as the birth date of the internet.

The internet before the web was a very different – and far less interesting – place to the one we're used to today. It was a series of linked military and academic systems, a world of arcane code used mainly by people with brains the size of planets and about as far from today's user-friendly sparkly multimedia experience as you can imagine. When most people say 'the internet' these days, they mean the web. Remarkably, for something that is so clearly identified with Silicon Valley and later dominated by West Coast start-ups, the web's (if not the internet's) origins are solidly Old World. Its father, Berners-Lee, was an Englishman working in a European research facility, and the world's first website, the catchily named info.cern. ch, wasn't a dotcom at all; it was .ch, which is the Swiss domain.

Berners-Lee was born in East Sheen, an unremarkable middle-class London suburb, in 1955. His upbringing was conventional enough – in fact, the only thing notable about his childhood was that both he and his parents were very bright. They were mathematicians who worked on some of the world's earliest computers such as the Ferranti Mark I. Tim was fascinated with electronics, and mealtime discussions included topics such as artificial intelligence and number games using imaginary numbers (the square roots of negative numbers). Berners-Lee went to school in Wandsworth, and then studied at Queen's College, Oxford, where he got a first in physics.

After graduating, he moved into software, working at Plessey Telecommunications for two years before moving to DG Nash Ltd; his contemporaries remember a man who was highly intelligent and very determined. Next, Berners-Lee became a freelance consultant, and this included a six-month contract at CERN, the enormous physics research facility in Geneva, in 1980. Wanting a way to link the information and various documents on his computer, he wrote a piece of software that was designed to organize information in a manner akin to the way the human mind does it. The idea he said was to 'keep track of all the random associations one comes across in real life'. It was called Enquire and, says Berners-Lee, 'formed the conceptual basis for the world wide web'. Essentially, Enquire meant that words in files could be linked to other files. It worked – although it was a far cry from today's globe-spanning hypertext, as it worked only on Berners-Lee's own computer.

From 1981 to 1984, he worked at John Poole's Image Computer Systems in technical design. In 1984, he returned to CERN as a fellow, and his interest in organizing information on computers was rekindled. At the time, this was a nightmare. The standardization and interoperability of today were a long way off, hardware and software varied hugely, and different machines often not only didn't speak the same language but had no interest in doing so. In 1989 Berners-Lee wrote a proposal for 'a large hypertext database with typed links', an idea that was received with polite indifference, although his boss, Mike Sendall, suggested he tried it out on a computer.

Berners-Lee found a more appreciative audience for his ideas in Robert Cailliau, a Belgian computer scientist, who was prepared to help him pitch for funding within CERN. When the two re-presented the idea to a conference in 1990 – talking about a web of documents that would be viewed in browsers and use a client server architecture – no one really got it either, so they went it alone. By the end of the year, Berners-Lee had everything he needed to build a basic web, although it would run only on a NeXT computer. (If it were possible to have a hyperlink here, there would be one to Steve Jobs.)

On 6 August 1991, he put the first website online. For those who are interested, it can still be found. The delightfully unassuming first paragraph reads: 'The WorldWideWeb (WWW) project aims to allow links to be made to any information anywhere. The address format includes an access method (=namespace), and for most name spaces a hostname and some sort of path.' Later on it says: 'The WWW project was started to allow high energy physicists to share data, news, and documentation. We are very interested in spreading the web to other areas, and having gateway servers for other data. Collaborators welcome.'

At this point, if Berners-Lee knew that what he was doing would one day (and not that far off) be compared to the invention of the printing press, he was being delightfully modest, but given the project's lacklustre past he may well have thought it would remain a useful academic tool, but little else. It's very easy to forget how difficult to navigate a lot of the web was back in the early days.

It's worth pointing out here too that the concept of hypertext wasn't actually Berners-Lee's own, but pre-dates him all the way to 1945. Nonetheless, it was his idea to put hypertext and the internet together. In the early 1990s, interest began to grow, and a few sites started to appear, although these were confined to science departments of universities and labs. In 1993, CERN released the web protocols and code for anyone's use, and in 1994 Berners-Lee established the World Wide Web Consortium (W3C) to implement standards for the web and maintain quality.

The year 1993 wasn't just the year that the protocols behind the web were made free though – the other highly significant milestone was the appearance of the Mosaic browser. Created by Marc Andreessen and Eric Bina, the browser is widely credited with popularizing the world wide web and bringing it within the reach of ordinary people. Indeed, although Mosaic lasted only from 1993 to 1997 it is still recognizable today as a web browser. Mosaic really was the last stage of the process kicked off by Berners-Lee in 1984. As anyone working or studying in the early 1990s will remember, at the start of the decade, for most people, there was no internet. A couple of years in and some very early adopters might have had e-mail, but it wasn't really until the mid-1990s (Internet Explorer first appeared in 1995) that things really took off and the web made its final transition from a tool for scientists to a bandwagon that every company wanted to be on. Amazon.com was launched in July 1995, just under four years after the first website appeared.

Berners-Lee is generally seen as a modest man and has more than once said that he was basically in the right place at the right time and noted that others were exploring the same ideas as him. All of this is true, but it is also unduly self-effacing. Many other great inventors in the past (such as Edison) were people heading up teams of researchers, whereas Berners-Lee really did come up with the web pretty much by himself. In this sense, he really did invent it – he is the lone genius of popular imagination. For all the people who helped implement, popularize and spread his invention, he alone came up with the idea. Of course, it wasn't just inventing it either. The other great thing he did – which is what puts him at odds with most of the rest of the people in this book – is that, having come up with something that would prove so fantastically useful and would underpin the great economic shift of the information economy, he simply gave it away. Berners-Lee has never made money directly from his invention.

His belief in the free interchange of information is something that is built into the very fabric of the web. Sometimes it's pretty much an unalloyed good like Wikipedia and blogging – and sometimes it's rather more mixed, such as file sharing and useful news sources discovering it's very, very hard to charge for information. More recently, Berners-Lee has been a tireless advocate of net neutrality, the principle that all information is equal and that ISPs do not favour certain sites and services over others. In 2004, he became a Professor of Computer Science at the University of Southampton, where he working on the semantic web. The idea behind this is that computers actually understand the information they are dealing with rather than simply serve it up to users. Late in 2009, he launched the World Wide Web Foundation. He may not have made money out of his invention, but he has been showered with honours. As well as the knighthood, he has a dozen honorary degrees and untold medals and awards and, in 2004, was voted the greatest living Briton. It is a fitting honour for a man who invented something so useful – and that in a little over a decade rewrote the way much of the world did business – and then simply gave it away.

References and further reading

Austin, Marcus (2001) Profile, *Business 2.0*

Berners-Lee, Tim, Biography from his own site

Johnson, Bobbie (2005) The Guardian profile: Tim Berners-Lee, *Guardian*, 12 August

Naughton, John (2003) The Observer profile – to serve us all his days, *Observer*, 19 April

Quittner, Joshua (1999) Network designer: Tim Berners-Lee, *Time*, 29 March

Chapter Seven
Anita Roddick

When Anita Roddick died in 2007, aged 64, the tributes poured in, but many of them were not from people you'd expect to be lauding a businesswoman. Along with Gordon Brown, the then UK Prime Minister, she was also praised by the Executive Director of Greenpeace and the Head of Amnesty International. And this, perhaps, is the key to who Roddick was. For although she built a hugely successful business empire of thousands of shops and amassed a considerable fortune, it's not for her business nous that she will be remembered. Rather, her place in history is assured because she was the first person really to fuse commerce and social activism. She recognized that business was one of the most powerful driving forces in the modern world – and she was determined to use it to further an environmental and ethical agenda. In this sense, Roddick is unusual – for her the business was a means to an end, rather than an end in itself.

In her field – socially responsible business – she was a pioneer in the truest sense. These days most people recycle, worry about indigenous people getting a fair deal and fret about their carbon footprints; any modern business worth its salt talks the talk of sustainability, multiple bottom lines and stakeholders. But if you cast your mind back to the early 1980s, to the heyday of Thatcher and Reagan, back then, for most businesspeople, green was a nice colour for a

Jaguar. Indeed, it's very easy to forget just how little most businesspeople cared about ethical matters then. It's not so much that they were callous (although there was a fair bit of that in Thatcher's Britain). Rather it was that it simply didn't figure on their agendas; they didn't care, because they didn't know. Of course, there was a green movement back then, but it was largely anti-business. Roddick's genius was to make ethics a high street proposition and use business as a force for good.

Anita Perilli was born on 23 October 1942 in a bomb shelter in Littlehampton, West Sussex, a town on England's south coast; the Body Shop still has its global HQ there. She was the daughter of Italian immigrants, and the only other Italian family in town were cousins. This, she said, made her 'a natural outsider – and I was drawn to other outsiders and rebels' (http://www.anitaroddick. com). James Dean was a hero, and she said that she developed an early sense of outrage: '[This] was awakened when I read a book about the Holocaust when I was ten.'

Like so many Italian immigrants at the time, her parents ran a café. When she was eight, they divorced, and her mother married her father's cousin, Henry. It turned out he was actually Anita's father, as her mother had been having an affair during the marriage; Anita was, she said, very pleased by this turn of events. Tragically, a year and a half after he married her mother Henry died.

After secondary school, Roddick trained as a teacher and then spent a year on a kibbutz in Israel. After that she went travelling to places as far-flung as the South Pacific islands and South Africa, where she was expelled for going to a jazz night at a black club. Here, perhaps, was the first foreshadowing of what was to come. She said that travelling helped develop her social conscience – although we might reasonably ask ourselves how many young women in the 1960s had well-developed social consciences. When she returned to the UK, her mother introduced her to a Scotsman called Gordon Roddick. 'Our bond was instant.' Indeed it was: she moved into his flat five days after meeting him, and the pair would spend almost 40 years together, until she died.

At 26, she gave birth to her first daughter, Justine; two years later she had Sam (who has followed loosely in her mother's footsteps, with an upmarket and ethical sex shop in London's Covent Garden, where hot sellers include sustainably harvested wooden dildos). Anita and Gordon married in 1970, when she was expecting Sam, and opened a restaurant and then a hotel.

The Body Shop was famously born out of necessity. In 1976, Gordon Roddick decided he wanted to ride a horse from Buenos Aires to Washington, DC (he abandoned the quest when the horse fell into a ravine). Prior to leaving, he helped his wife arrange a £4,000 loan, the idea being that she would start a business to support herself and her daughters. At the time, she said, she had little idea what retail really involved, but she did have 'a wealth of experience' from her travels. She'd seen first-hand the beauty rituals and products used by women in pre-industrial societies, of which there were still plenty in the 1960s and 1970s, and she'd been influenced by growing up in wartime and post-war Britain, with rationing and austerity, where everything was reused. She opened up in Brighton's picturesque Lanes in 1976, selling a very limited range of products she'd made at home. By the time her husband returned from his horse-riding expedition, 11 months later, she had a second shop.

There is some confusion about how green and ethical the Body Shop was when it started out, but what seems pretty clear is that the products were always fairly natural and that Roddick was deeply against animal testing – and it's also worth remembering that the yardsticks for this sort of thing barely existed in the late 1970s. What is clear though is that Roddick's customers loved her simple, cruelty-free products and voted with their feet; in 1978, the company opened its first overseas outlet (a kiosk in Brussels), and by the 1980s the chain had become a British high street icon, albeit one that was curiously out of sync with the ethos of Thatcher's Britain.

In 1984, it was floated on London's unlisted securities market (the stock market's junior market, which was supplanted by AIM). It moved to a full listing the following year. Body Shop being a PLC was a rude awakening for Roddick. As she later said, 'I should never have gone public, but you couldn't know at the time.' Quite simply, her idea of a company with multiple bottom lines and stakeholders was about 15 years ahead of its time, and the City was interested in only one thing – the real bottom line. She fell out with her CEO, Patrick Gournay, the company struggled in the United States, and the whole experience imbued in her a deep distrust of the business-as-usual corporate world and of business journalists. Nonetheless, the company's shares actually did very well, and in 1990 the company was valued at £800 million, making her the UK's fourth-richest woman; she owned 30 per cent.

But Roddick's activism was always more interesting. In 1985, she threw the company behind saving whales; in 1989, she wanted to save rainforests; and in 1990 she campaigned against animal testing. The company collected signatures for human rights campaigns. Rather than buy products like cocoa butter and brazil nuts on the commodities markets, Roddick would go out and meet the growers in places like Central America, India and the Amazon and deal direct with them, ensuring they got a better price for their goods. In 1986, the Body Shop launched its first community trade product, a footsie roller, made by a supplier in southern India. In 1990, the charity the Body Shop Foundation was established – the *Big Issue* magazine, which provides a source of income for homeless people, was one of its early projects. The Body Shop famously never had a marketing department – and with Anita Roddick at its helm there's a good argument that it never really needed one. Whether she was railing against multinationals, espousing feminist philosophy or getting gassed at the WTO riots in 1999, she was never far from the public eye.

But the 1990s were less kind to the Body Shop. The Roddicks continued to struggle with the City and said they would have taken the company private again if they could have afforded to do so. The characteristics that made her such a great face for the brand didn't endear her to the money people, and like many businesses the Body Shop discovered that it's easy to be cute when you're small, but rather harder when you're a multinational. Criticism wasn't confined to those in pinstripes either – in 1994, the journalist Jon Entine wrote a damning piece about the Body Shop in the magazine *Business Ethics* and, it seemed, there were plenty of others who were prepared to point the finger too.

With the benefit of hindsight, this is perhaps a little unfair. It's true that the company didn't always live up to its lofty ambitions, but it's also true that in the main it was trying to do the right thing – and that if you trade on being green then the tiniest environmental infraction's going to get noticed. Mistakes were made, but many of these were because the company was blazing a trail rather than following a well-trodden path – and, as Roddick noted, the Body Shop was often held to far higher standards than others. An example of the kind of back and forth she had with her detractors comes from this Jon Entine piece published in the *Daily Mail*. Etine wrote:

> For the first and only time, I was allowed to ask her a question. I cited a version of her speech, given in 1993, in which she called for a boycott of China. 'How do you square your call for a boycott when The Body Shop sources dozens of products from China? According to fair trade organisations, you have personally rebuffed pleas to switch to more ethical sources.' She shot me a look. 'You just don't understand, do you? I was talking about what business should do, not what we actually do. My job is to inspire. But we have a bloody business to run.'

It's interesting here that he called Roddick out over China, as the world's most exciting new economy has proved a stumbling block for numerous companies with an ethical dimension. Over a decade later Google would find itself in a similar position over Chinese requests for censorship and government-sanctioned snooping on accounts. And, for all the shrill voices of single-issue groups, it's a dilemma with no easy answer. It's not just that profits and doing the right thing may lie in diametrically opposed directions; it's also that sometimes the right thing is far from clear.

However, the Body Shop's problems weren't just down to growing pains. Back in the early 1980s, what Roddick was doing was genuinely fresh and unusual, whereas in 1997 everyone was doing it – and in some cases they were probably doing it in a fresher and more interesting way than the Body Shop. When the first Lush shops started appearing in the 1990s, suddenly the Body Shop started to look like part of the establishment it had once railed against.

In 2006, the Body Shop was sold to the French cosmetics giant L'Oréal, a move that some of the company's oldest fans never really forgave it for – not least because L'Oréal is a far more conventional cosmetics company, with all that entails. However, the Body Shop is managed independently, and being sold to a multinational looking for an ethical addition to its portfolio is a fate that befalls a lot of socially responsible businesses – the chocolatiers Green & Black's are now owned by Cadbury (which is owned by Kraft), and the hippy ice-cream company Ben & Jerry's belongs to the Anglo-Dutch conglomerate Unilever. True believers might think this is selling out, but it's also arguable that becoming part of these groups exposes more people to the ideas and principles behind ethical businesses.

Sadly Roddick didn't have much time left. She'd been diagnosed with cirrhosis of the liver. She'd developed this as a result of contracting hepatitis C 30 years earlier from a blood transfusion she'd had after giving birth to her second daughter, and had been unaware of it until she was diagnosed in 2004. Characteristically, when she discovered she had the disease, she began campaigning to raise awareness of it and help others, rather than dwelling on her own predicament. As she said when she announced it in early 2007, 'It's a bit of a bummer, but you groan and move on.' She died in September 2007 of a brain haemorrhage. In 2008 it was revealed that she had left none of her £51 million fortune to her family and friends; rather she'd given the lot to various charities.

Her greatest legacy was cultural rather than financial though. She changed for ever the idea of what business is capable of doing – and what it's there for. Nowadays even companies who make weapons worry about social responsibility (or at least pretend to). This is in no small part down to Anita Roddick.

References and further reading

Anita Roddick website
BBC News (2007) Dame Anita Roddick dies aged 64, 10 September
Body Shop website
Entine, J (1994) Shattered Image: Is the Body Shop Too Good to be True?, in *Business Ethics*, (October 1994), 23–28
McCarthy, Michael (2007) How Anita changed the world, *Independent*, 12 September
Moore, Matthew (2008) Anita Roddick's will reveals she donated entire £51m fortune to charity, *Telegraph*, 16 April
Roddick, Anita, Biography, website
Roddick, Gordon (2007) I want to do Anita justice, *Telegraph*, 21 October
Siegle, Lucy (2007) Profile: Anita Roddick ('And this time, it's personal'), *Observer*, 19 February
Telegraph (2007) Obituary of Anita Roddick, 12 September

Chapter Eight
Ray Kroc

If ever there was a man for whom the cheesy epithet 'a legend in his own lunchtime' was invented, it was Ray Kroc. He has (quite accurately) been called the Henry Ford of hamburgers and the father of fast food. It is a testament to his incredible success that the chain whose growth he kick-started is now used as shorthand for globalization – by both its boosters and its detractors – and that many aspects of multinationals we take for granted first appeared in his business.

As with all truly influential businesspeople, Kroc's impact has gone far beyond the world of commerce, and McDonald's has a place in popular culture few even aspire too. The *Economist* publishes an alternative exchange rate table called the Big Mac Index, and the term 'McJob' recently made it into the *Oxford English Dictionary*; while McDonald's made a big fuss about the term denigrating the employment opportunities it offers people, one suspects they were secretly delighted. And it's all down to a man who looked as though he was going to finish his career selling milkshake machines.

Ray Kroc was, by any standards, a very late bloomer. His involvement in the world's largest food chain started when he was in his 50s, at an age when most people are thinking about retirement rather than revolutionizing the food industry, people's diets and the

US landscape. Kroc was born in 1902 in Illinois. In 1917, he'd attempted to become an ambulance driver in the First World War (he lied about his age), but during his training the war ended and he stayed on US soil. Needing work, he played piano, before beginning work for the Lily Tulip Cup Company in 1922 selling cups and paper products.

In the course of his life as a travelling salesman, Kroc encountered Earl Prince, a client who had invented the 'multimixer', a device that could blend five milkshakes at once. Kroc, now 37, saw the machine's potential and obtained exclusive marketing rights to it. He then spent the next 17 years travelling around the country selling multimixers to drug-store owners and restaurants. In the 1950s, though, sales began to fall. The great suburbanization of the United States had begun, and mom-and-pop soda fountains were closing in their droves; Kroc's business was in steep and apparently terminal decline. However, bucking this downward trend was a restaurant in San Bernardino, California, that had ordered an extraordinary eight multimixers – meaning it needed to churn 40 milkshakes at a time. Kroc was intrigued.

Richard and Maurice McDonald had left New England in 1930, drawn to California by the bright lights of Hollywood. Their dreams of riches hadn't quite panned out, and they'd founded a restaurant in San Bernardino, then a rather nowhere town 65 miles east of Los Angeles. When Kroc visited he was amazed by what he saw. Thanks to the 'speedee service' system the brothers had introduced in 1948, the restaurant was a hive of well-organized activity, with food being prepared in a manner analogous to Henry Ford's assembly line. The menu had been pared down to nine items, and food was served on paper plates and with plastic utensils; there was no seating. Prices were extraordinarily low, and orders were fulfilled within 60 seconds. In an era when restaurant hygiene was often lacking and workers were sloppy, the place was a sparkling testament to cleanliness and efficiency. Kroc later wrote in his autobiography, 'I felt like some latter day Newton who'd just had an Idaho potato caromed off his skull.' He believed that he had seen the future and that the future was a McDonald's at every busy junction.

The following day Kroc put his vision to the brothers, but they weren't particularly interested. They'd already experimented with expansion and sold a few franchises, but ultimately they were making a very comfortable living from their business and saw no need to work any harder. Kroc, however, was a true believer and, using powers of persuasion honed by decades of selling experience, managed to talk the brothers into giving exclusive rights to sell their model. Kroc would sell the franchises for $950. On top of this, he would receive 1.9 per cent of gross sales for each franchise, of which 0.5 per cent would go to the brothers. Kroc opened his first McDonald's near Chicago to serve as a model and a billboard to would-be franchisees.

Interestingly, many people assume that Kroc came up with the original idea of McDonald's, but as we've seen this was not the case – the concept and much of the early branding were the brothers'. However, it is still absolutely right to see Kroc and not them as the man behind McDonald's. Without Kroc, McDonald's would almost certainly be another (probably long-defunct) minor restaurant chain that no one had heard of.

What Kroc had – and the brothers lacked – was the drive to turn a small business into a globe-spanning colossus. Indeed, Kroc is possibly the clearest example of the business truism that having a good idea really isn't enough – he is the living embodiment of Edison's famous quote: 'Genius is 1 per cent inspiration and 99 per cent perspiration.' With McDonald's, the brothers supplied the 1 per cent. One of the reasons for Kroc's extraordinary drive may have been that, by 1955, Kroc had no plan B – although the multimixers had provided him with a good income, the writing was on the wall and he wasn't getting any younger. McDonald's really was his last roll of the dice.

Kroc was a stickler for regulation and uniformity – and saw this as the key to success – so he set about perfecting the brothers' model. Everything was standardized, from the beef patties to the fries and the milkshakes, down to an eighth of an inch and a quarter of an ounce. Rather than implement the relatively complex training a short order chef required, Kroc broke everything down into simple tasks that anyone could do with minimal training. This is why the comparison with Henry Ford is so apt. Before Kroc, fast food had been a relatively slapdash process that required trained workers and resulted in a variable product. Kroc changed all that with his particular vision of perfection. He believed that wherever you ate in the United States you should have exactly the same food and experience, from Florida to Alaska.

He was an innovator in other ways too. In an era when food was still seen as an art, he brought scientific rigour to the process even to the point of building a laboratory. He attacked costs ruthlessly to keep prices down and was an early employer of part-timers and teenagers. Breaking jobs down into components and setting up teams in kitchens helped with this. He was a great believer in quality too – in an era when many burgers where bulked with cheap filler, he insisted on the now famous all-beef patties. He also scouted for new suburban locations for his restaurants with a strategic zeal that mixed economics and town planning.

Of course when Kroc started out, he didn't have the field to himself. Other fledgling chains existed. But Kroc wanted McDonald's to be different. One way he achieved this was through the cleanliness and uniformity of his restaurants. The other was the relationships he had with his franchisees, for while Kroc may have deskilled the jobs of those who worked in the restaurants he treated those who owned them rather better. Many businesses at the time viewed franchisees as little more than cash cows who were there to be milked for as much money as possible. Kroc treated them far better. He wanted to sell them a restaurant that was like a functioning factory – and he wanted to work with them, rather than wring every cent he could out of them. Furthermore, although Kroc was religious about uniformity, he allowed franchisees a great deal of latitude to experiment and innovate within the framework, and he genuinely listened to their ideas. Many of the company's products, such as the filet-o-fish, the egg McMuffin and even the iconic Big Mac, were invented by individual franchisees. For Kroc, when he sold a McDonald's franchise, he started a long-term business relationship.

Here it sounds as though Kroc was on the fast track to success. In fact, he had a serious problem. For all its healthy numbers in terms of growth, at this stage the company was not doing very well financially. The deal that Kroc had cut with the McDonald brothers was not a good one for him and meant that, while turnover was huge in the early 1960s, he was making virtually nothing himself. Worse still, Kroc's obsessiveness was rubbing uneasily against the brothers' indifference. He desperately wanted to buy them out, as he felt their approach was a drag on the brand.

Long-term salvation for Kroc came in the form of a very smart lawyer with a very elegant solution, Harry J. Sonneborn. This was for the company to become its franchisees' landlord. In 1956, the Franchise Realty Corporation was founded. The idea was that this company would buy sites and then lease them to McDonald's franchisees; the franchisees would pay the parent company either a fee or a percentage of their turnover, whichever was larger. It was a masterstroke, and Kroc would later credit Sonneborn as being the man responsible for turning the company around. As the book *McDonald's behind the Arches* (Love, 1995) says, 'What converted McDonald's into a money machine had nothing to do with Ray Kroc or the McDonald brothers or even the popularity of McDonald's hamburgers, French fries, and milk shakes. Rather, McDonald's made its money on real estate and on a little-known formula developed by Harry J. Sonneborn.' Indeed, although Kroc never agreed with this view, Sonneborn once told a group of investors that the company was actually in real estate business: 'The only reason we sell 15 cent hamburgers is because they are the greatest provider of revenue from which our tenants can pay us rent.'

But while Franchise Realty would ultimately rescue Kroc, it was going to take a few years and he wasn't out of the woods. In 1961, a particularly grim year for Kroc, his marriage ended in divorce – his wife of 39 years felt the company left no space for her. Further, having given several valuable employees large chunks of stock because he couldn't afford big salaries, Kroc was forced to give up a further 22 per cent of the stock in order to secure a loan.

Even this wasn't enough. He'd reached the point where he would do virtually anything to get rid of 'his' chain's founders, who often seemed to be working to undermine what he'd done. Eventually they came to an agreement. The brothers demanded $1 million tax free each, which equalled $2.7 million; Kroc managed to raise the money, but on onerous terms. Although in retrospect it was a terrible deal for the McDonalds, at the time Kroc thought he'd paid a very high price. They'd also fallen out over whether the deal included the original restaurant or not. Eventually the brothers got to keep it, but had to change the name, which they did, to 'The Big M'. Kroc opened a McDonald's across the street and drove it out of business.

Finally Kroc had the business he wanted. By the mid-1960s the company had hundreds of outlets across the United States and, in 1965, it went public, giving it the cash to expand in a booming but increasingly competitive market. It also started advertising, and before long was running national adverts, which were hugely expensive but also hugely effective. Ronald McDonald, who had first appeared in the early 1960s, was joined by a veritable community of characters, including Grimace, Mayor McCheese and the Hamburglar; of these, only Ronald now remains.

In the 1970s, McDonald's became the largest single fast food chain in the United States, and in 1971 it moved into Germany and Japan. In 1977, it opened its first London store. Kroc became a figure on the national stage, bought the San Francisco Padres, a baseball team, and met presidents. The company also started to attract criticism – both from those who were concerned about the perceived nutritional failings of its food and from those who were concerned about the United States' shift from a manufacturing to a service economy.

None of this really troubled Kroc though. He remained largely unaffected by wealth and the power it brought, outside the immediate sphere of the Golden Arches; he also resisted the temptation to gentrify himself. He stepped down as CEO in 1968, although he remained heavily – and in some ways quite obsessively – involved in the organization until his death in 1984, aged 81.

By the time of his death, his company had sold nearly 50 billion hamburgers and was one of the biggest companies in the United States, with a value of around $4 billion, but Kroc's influence on the world was far greater than this. Indeed, if you want a company that embodies a huge number of the economic shifts that took place in the second half of the 20th century you could do far worse than McDonald's. More than that, though, McDonald's changed the way the United States ate, it changed the way Americans worked, it changed the US landscape and, you could even argue, it changed the way some Americans looked. Few business thinkers have had such a great impact outside the world of business.

References and further reading

Entrepreneur.com, Biography of Ray Kroc, www.entrepreneur.com
Gross, Daniel (1996) *Forbes Greatest Business Stories of All Time*, pp 232–45
Kroc, Ray (1990) *Grinding It Out: The making of McDonald's*
Love, John F (1995) *McDonald's behind the Arches*, Bantam Press
McDonald's website, www.mcdonalds.com
Pace, Eric (1984) Obituary, *New York Times*, 15 January
Pepin, Jaques (1998) Burger meister, Ray Kroc, *Time*, 7 December
Schlosser, Eric (2001) *Fast Food Nation*

Chapter Nine
Rupert Murdoch

Murdoch is often – perhaps even usually – portrayed as a kind of Montgomery Burns of the media. This is not entirely unfair, as he is not only rich, but wields enormous power and influence via a network of newspapers and television stations ranging from the *Sun* (the UK's bestselling daily paper) to Fox News (the controversial ring-wing US channel). Even *The Simpsons*, the world's longest-running cartoon, is part of Murdoch's empire, and in 1999 he made a guest appearance, perhaps to cock a snook at those who say he has no sense of humour.

But, as much as the man himself, there is also the legend that Murdoch has carefully cultivated over the years. He's a figure who inspires strong feelings – many loathe him. The reasons given are usually that he is responsible for dumbing down and vulgarity in the media and that he exercises a malign influence over politics in the countries he operates in. The British playwright Dennis Potter, when terminally ill, memorably said 'I will call my cancer Rupert' (BBC, 2002); Alan Bennett refused an honorary degree from Oxford because of its links to Murdoch; and the satirical magazine *Private Eye* routinely pillories him as 'the dirty digger'. Yet there are very few heads of state who would refuse a request for a meeting with Murdoch. And, as we shall see, in the final analysis his influence on the media may be altogether less malign than many think.

Keith Rupert Murdoch was born in Melbourne, Australia in 1931. His father, Keith, ran a regional newspaper group, News Ltd, and the family were comfortably off. He read philosophy, politics and economics (PPE – the degree of choice for many of the UK's elite) at Oxford, and when his father died in 1953 he inherited the family firm. He soon established himself as a savvy media operator and expanded far beyond his regional base, becoming a powerful force in Australian newspapers. Before long, he was looking abroad, and buying titles in New Zealand. In 1964, he launched the *Australian*, the country's first national daily. The *Australian* prefigured much of what was to come. It was of course a business venture, but as a broadsheet (ie quality) paper it was also designed to give Murdoch political influence.

A small country (in terms of population and economy) like Australia couldn't hold Murdoch for long, though, so he turned his sights on the UK. His first really big acquisition abroad was the salacious UK Sunday paper the *News of the World*, which he gained control of in 1969 after an acrimonious battle with Robert Maxwell, another larger-than-life press magnate. The same year, he bought the *Sun*, although at the time it was a broadsheet and a far cry from the bellicose 'red top' that embodies tabloid journalism today. Ever the businessman, Murdoch did so partly because the presses he'd acquired with the *News of the World* were doing nothing six days out of seven. After buying the *Sun*, Murdoch relaunched it as a tabloid, the infamous page three that featured topless models appeared a year later, and in 1979 the transformation was complete when the paper dropped its Labour allegiances and put its (by then considerable) support behind Margaret Thatcher. Two years later, in 1981, Murdoch caused a furore in the UK when he bought those pillars of the establishment, *The Times* and *The Sunday Times*. Naturally, his critics were worried about what he'd do to them; Murdoch certainly had plans, but they weren't what many expected.

In the mid-1980s, in response to the ongoing labour disputes on Fleet Street, Murdoch sacked 6,000 striking workers and moved his four titles to Wapping in East London's docklands. The industrial dispute and protests went on for a year, but it was Murdoch who won in the end; unlike the strikers, he was sufficiently well prepared (and financially cushioned) to be able to afford simply to sit the strike out. The Wapping dispute was a key episode in the decline in power of the trade unions in Margaret Thatcher's Britain. It also changed the face of Fleet Street and the balance of power in the papers. By the late 1980s, almost all of Britain's national newspapers had left their traditional home for the docklands, and Murdoch's model of printing was being widely adopted.

Britain and print weren't big enough to hold Murdoch's ambitions either. He'd also been looking at the biggest market of all. In the early 1970s, he'd picked up a local US newspaper and the checkout tabloid the *Star*. In 1976, however, he raised his sights and bought the *New York Post*, promising to maintain its traditions and then promptly turning it into the sensationalist right-wing tabloid we know today.

He was also looking beyond print, doubtless realizing that the power of papers was waning and that television was playing an ever more important role in shaping agendas. In 1983, he took over the ailing satellite broadcaster Satellite Television UK, which was relaunched the following year as Sky Channel. In 1990, this merged with its rival BSB to form British Sky Broadcasting, with Murdoch's News International as a majority shareholder. The company bled cash in its early years, but it was subsidized by the rest of News International (Murdoch has never had an issue with profitable parts of the business supporting their unprofitable cousins). By 1992, it had secured the rights to broadcast Premier League football and, since the mid-1990s, has been largely profitable and a big player in the UK's TV market. Its chairman is currently James Murdoch, Rupert Murdoch's son.

Murdoch was also increasingly active in other areas of entertainment too. In 1985, he bought first half and then the whole of TCF, 20th Century Fox's holding corporation, and began acquiring television stations, with the idea of forming a fourth US television network to rival ABC, NBC and CBS. In 1985, he became a US citizen, as only citizens are allowed to own TV stations in the United States. In the early days Fox Television copped a fair amount of criticism for the trashiness of its shows, but it built its audience and also gained credibility with shows such as *The OC* and *House*. In 1996, it launched the channel for which it is perhaps best known: Fox News. To say that the news channel has been controversial is like saying Murdoch is ambitious. Launched by former Republican Party strategist Roger Ailes, the self-proclaimed 'Fair and balanced' news channel rode high in the Bush years with its right-wing populist slant.

For US moderates and the left, however, Fox was a disaster, as it finally gave the right-wing grassroots their own news channel and something approaching a coherent voice, and it became hugely influential. The channel has often been accused of a blatant right-wing bias and misrepresenting facts to suit its agenda, but in the United States' polarized politics complaints from the left tend to be red meat for the right, and Fox and its presenters have revelled in the opprobrium heaped upon it by its *bien pensant* detractors. It's worth noting, however, that Murdoch is very much a straw who bends with the wind. After Obama's victory he made some careful moves to distance himself from both the channel's political slant and the outspoken Ailes.

Of course, with Murdoch nearing his ninth decade, there's plenty of speculation about his legacy, especially as the structure of the inheritance is a Byzantine one, with different voting rights for children by different marriages, who range from under 10 to middle-aged. However, Murdoch does not show any real signs of giving up. Indeed, Murdoch's appetite for influence and hunger for deals are undiminished, although it is said that his newest wife has mellowed his politics somewhat. His apparent immortality – or belief in his immortality – can manifest itself in the strangest ways. In 2008, his biographer Michael Wolff said that the mogul's hair colour ranges from flaming orange to aubergine and then went on to explain that the multibillionaire dyes his hair himself over the sink.

The 2000s have been more of a mixed decade for Murdoch, with some interesting reversals of the norm. As with all papers, his stable have suffered from both declining circulation and ad revenues and the rise of the net, meaning that where once profitable papers subsidized satellite TV now the reverse is true. He's also had some decidedly mixed encounters with the new economy. Most notably, in 2005, he bought Myspace for $580 million. Initially this looked like a shrewd move into new media, and the advertising revenues looked handsome, although in recent years the success of Facebook has led many to suggest that, rather than having made a smart buy, Murdoch had bought a site that was on the turn. This and his recent spats with Google (he and News Corp executives have repeatedly described the search engine as a 'parasite' that profits from content created by others) have led some to suggest that Murdoch does not in fact understand the internet and that these are the rantings of an old man watching the empire he built turn to sand.

Even his still profitable papers aren't what they once were. In the early 1990s the *Sun* used to boast – and many believed – that it had the power to swing UK elections, but just as it was at its most bellicose its influence was peaking. In 1992, it famously backed the Tories in the UK general election (and stuck the knife into Labour), proclaiming afterwards 'It's the Sun wot won it'. Within a few years its circulation had peaked at just under 5 million. The figure is now just over 3 million and, in the last UK general election, the party that it backed, rather than winning an overall majority, had to go into coalition with the Liberal Democrats – a result that speaks volumes.

But there are other, very good reasons not to write Murdoch off. His most recent significant US acquisition was the *Wall Street Journal* in 2007. Here, many feared, he would destroy one of the United States' few remaining successful serious papers, but to their surprise he seems to have reinvigorated it. Indeed, as the UK media commentator Roy Greenslade (*Time*, 28 June 2007) says, Murdoch seems to take a more hands-off approach to his serious papers, while cheerfully meddling in his tabloids. The *Wall Street Journal* is a real jewel in Murdoch's crown and one he overpaid for. It is thought that Murdoch may now aim squarely at the *New York Times*, probably the most influential paper in the world and the ultimate vindication for a man many see as a philistine. A *New York Magazine* article printed in early 2010 said: 'Some see an Ahab-like obsession in Murdoch's pursuit of the *Times*. "[Buying the *Journal*] was the worst deal he ever did. It never made sense," a former senior News Corp. executive says. "He had no justification for why he should buy it – he just wanted it"' (Sherman, 2010).

Those who think that age will lessen Murdoch's appetite for deals and empire building should probably look to the past for a guide to the future; it seems likely that the only thing that will stop him is the grave or an illness leading to the grave. He is the archetypal tycoon for whom enough is never enough. It's always about the next move and the next deal.

For all Murdoch's activity in the United States, however, what is happening on the other side of the Atlantic is just as interesting, if not more so. His latest tactics aim to address the problem that the internet has brought to the newspaper markets – globally, but in the United States and the UK in particular. As titles around the world have struggled with the simultaneous problems of declining ad revenues and the fact that they are giving their content away free online, Murdoch alone has recently started to charge for mainstream titles.

From June 2010, the *Times* and the *Sunday Times* (two of the UK's best-known and most widely read 'quality' papers) started to charge online readers for content. This is an extraordinarily bold move, as the only papers that have made this model work so far are the *Financial Times* and the *Wall Street Journal*, both of which might be considered special cases (business news is a specialist area, and companies are often happy to pay subscriptions). But with the *Times* Murdoch is competing with three other UK broadsheets (and possibly the *Daily Mail*), all of which offer a broadly similar product and all of which are free. He is betting that where he goes others will follow. If he's right, the man whom so many have castigated for ruining newspapers over the years may just turn out to be their saviour.

Time magazine described Murdoch as 'both the latest and the last of the outsized media moguls... men who loved their properties and used them to make fortunes and influence politics and society', but, the article said, 'unlike his contemporaries, Murdoch has been able to consistently see round the corner' (Pooley, 2007). This is probably about as accurate a two-line summary of Murdoch as you'll get and one that those who write him off would do well to remember.

References and further reading

BBC profile, Rupert Murdoch
BBC (2002) Interview with Dennis Potter, 31 June
Pooley, Eric (2007) Exclusive: Rupert Murdoch speaks, *Time*, 28 June
Robinson, James (2007) Rupert Murdoch, protector of the printed word, *Observer*, 9 August
Sherman, Gabriel (2010) The raging septuagenarian, *New York Magazine*, 8 March
Sydney Morning Herald (2010) Murdoch told: live and let dye go, 9 March
Walker, Andrew (2002) Rupert Murdoch: bigger than Kane, *BBC*, 31 July
Wolff, Michael (2008) Tuesday with Rupert, *Vanity Fair*, October

Chapter Ten
Peter Drucker

When Peter Drucker died in 2005, aged 95, the tributes flowed in. Jack Welch said, 'The world knows he was the greatest management thinker of the last century', while the management guru Tom Peters described him as 'the creator and inventor of modern management'. These two pretty much set the tone: there was almost no one who had a bad word for Peter Drucker – and he drew followers from all walks of life. Fans ranged from Karl Rove and George W Bush to Intel's Andy Grove, Winston Churchill and Bill Gates.

When Drucker began philosophizing about management in the late 1940s and early 1950s, modern management as a discipline didn't really exist and managers didn't have the toolkit they needed to deal with the burgeoning number of multinational corporations. Drucker gave them that, but his story is much more too. It is the history of the modern corporation itself (he coined the terms 'knowledge workers' and 'management by objective'), and his tale follows Western capitalism from the halcyon days of the 1950s and 1960s to the disillusionment, cynicism and self-interest of the 2000s.

Drucker is something of an oddity in management. In a field that is notoriously prone to fads and fashion (largely, one suspects, because of the scarcity of truly hard, predictive theories), Drucker's thinking is revered and continues to be revered; indeed Drucker himself saw management not as a science but as a liberal art. It's not difficult (especially after the banking crisis) to find people who'll tell you that Drucker is as relevant as he's ever been. Of course, not everything he said or wrote was great – and some of it was total nonsense – but, as the *Economist* once noted, 'Even when he was wrong, he had a way of being thought provoking.'

He was also a consummate intellectual and something of a polymath, and the vast body of knowledge he collected across any number of fields both informed and illuminated his management thinking and made what he said all the more compelling. He was legendary for the breadth of his cultural influences: it wasn't unusual to find him citing references from Byzantium to Jane Austen. Five years after his death, he still commands a cult-like following. There are Peter Drucker societies all over the world. Conferences continue to be held to discuss his significance, and books about him continue to be published.

Much of what made Drucker was his background. He was born in 1909 in Vienna, when the city was a major cultural hub. His father was a senior civil servant, and his mother had studied medicine. It was an upper-middle-class house full of intellectuals, and he met Sigmund Freud as a child; the economist Joseph Schumpeter was a family friend. This early exposure to giants in so many fields is widely credited with turning him into something of a Renaissance man. His biographer Jack Beatty (2005) would write, 'Like Conrad's "Mr. Kurtz," all Europe went into the making of Peter Drucker.'

After graduating from the local academic school, Drucker moved to Hamburg, where he worked as clerk, while studying in the evenings at Hamburg University. In 1929, he found employment at the Frankfurt branch of a Wall Street firm and transferred to Frankfurt University. He also joined the city's largest daily paper (the *Frankfurter General-Anzeiger*) as a financial journalist; a year later he was head of foreign affairs and business (although his career also included editing the women's page). Despite his youth, he even interviewed Hitler. In 1931, he gained a doctorate in international law at the age of 22. A year later he published a pamphlet on Friedrich Julius Stahl, a German conservative philosopher disapproved of by the Nazis. It was designed to antagonize, and it did. The Nazi government banned it and burnt copies. Very shortly afterwards Drucker realized he needed to leave Germany and moved to the UK.

He found work as a securities analyst in London and, while in the UK, he attended John Maynard Keynes's lectures at Cambridge. This awakened an important realization – that, while economists were interested in the behaviour of currencies, commodities and so on, he was interested in how people acted. Drucker was not greatly enamoured of London. He found it backward looking, and it reminded him too much of Vienna. In 1937 he moved to the United States to act as a correspondent for a group of papers.

In 1939 he published his first book, *The End of Economic Man: The origins of totalitarianism*. Three years later, he joined Bennington College, Vermont as Professor of Politics and Philosophy. In 1943, he published a second book, *The Future of Industrial Man*. This brought him to the attention of General Motors (GM), which invited him to spend two years studying the company. GM opened its doors to Drucker – from the shop floor to the boardroom, he was given access. When Drucker proposed that he might write a book about management, his sponsors at GM were surprised: they didn't believe that anyone would read it. One of his sponsors said, 'I don't see anyone interested in a book on management.' The book that resulted, *The Concept of the Corporation*, was Drucker's springboard to greatness. Although it introduced many new concepts, the two most important were empowerment and the idea of knowledge workers. With the first, the command and control model was starting to look a bit long in the tooth, decentralization was catching on, and Drucker was the man to articulate how in order for it to work you had to free up individual members of staff. With the latter, he anticipated the shift from grunt work to brain work in the advanced economies of the West. The book was a bestseller, although interestingly GM's then Chairman, Alfred Sloan, hated it, to the point that he refused to acknowledge its existence.

In 1950, Drucker became Professor of Management at New York University Business School, and in 1954 he published *The Practice of Management*. This set out three of his best-known precepts: What is our business? Who is our customer? What does our customer consider value? The book is also credited with introducing the idea of management by objective. Drucker became well known for his predictions – it was in the 1950s that he said that IT would change the face of business and that Japan would become a global economic superpower. This sounds unremarkable now, but it was back when Japan was widely seen as a maker of second-rate goods – and, what is more, Drucker also predicted the country's post-1990 slump.

Throughout the 1960s Drucker continued to teach and publish at New York University, eventually earning the University's Presidential Citation, its highest award. In 1971, he moved to Claremont Graduate School in California, and in 1975 he started the column he would write for the *Wall Street Journal* for 20 years. Between 1970 and 1980, he also averaged just under a book a year – this he described as his period of greatest productivity. Perhaps most impressively, in 1974 sales of his book *Management: Tasks, responsibilities, practices* overtook Dr Alex Comfort's *The Joy of Sex*. By now Drucker was being hailed as a guru, but he used to joke: 'I have been saying for many years that we are using the word "guru" only because "charlatan" is too long to fit into a headline.'

Drucker was also a consultant who worked with many household names of the post-war United States. Companies such as GE, Coca-Cola, IBM and Intel were put under his microscope, and he was always ready to offer frank advice for where they were getting it wrong, but he usually did so in way that suggested understanding and empathy, rather than confrontation. He also worked with governments and non-profit organizations, often for nothing, and foresaw the rise of the non-profit organization as a way of providing a form of satisfaction that most companies failed to provide. It was in the 1980s too that Drucker started to notice another disturbing trend – executive greed. As *Businessweek* wrote (Byrne, 2005):

> In a 1984 essay he persuasively argued that CEO pay had rocketed out of control and implored boards to hold CEO compensation to no more than 20 times what the rank and file made. What particularly enraged him was the tendency of corporate managers to reap massive earnings while firing thousands of their workers. 'This is morally and socially unforgivable,' wrote Drucker, 'and we will pay a heavy price for it.'

This might be seen as the beginnings of a disenchantment with managers that grew towards the end of his life. As executive compensation mushroomed and the idea that business should have a purpose beyond just profits withered, Drucker became bitterly disillusioned. He believed that poor-quality managers were being rewarded excessively as they slashed and burnt their way through workforces. Drucker had always held managers up as heroic. Now he was criticizing them, and they no longer liked what they heard.

This is probably why, in the hyper-capitalism of the late 1990s and early 2000s, some started to dismiss Drucker as a man whose time was past. In 1997, he said, 'In the next economic downturn, there will be an outbreak of bitterness and contempt for the super chieftains who pay themselves millions.' He was half-right – there was an outbreak of contempt and bitterness, although he failed to foresee quite how unfocused and how misplaced this rage would be. Nonetheless, the crisis made many who had had doubts realize that it was Drucker, not CEOs, who was right. Moreover, he walked the talk and, despite the wealth that his work had brought him, had little time for materialism. Those who visited him at home often remarked on how modestly he lived. Drucker died in 2005 of natural causes, just before his 96th birthday. He continued to work and publish up until the end – in fact, his last book came out after his death.

Of course, Drucker wasn't perfect. As Simon Caulkin (2005), the *Observer*'s then management editor, wrote in his obituary:

> Among his other firsts, he invented not only the importance of management but also, perhaps inevitably, the importance of managers – with less favourable consequences. As Chris Grey of Judge Business School points out, Drucker was uniquely of his time and place, and when in the 1950s and 1960s he held up to corporate managers the flattering mirror of themselves as new cultural and economic heroes, they were dazzled by what they saw.

Other criticisms widely seen as fair include the charge that he was far better on large organizations than small ones, to the point where he more or less ignored them, and that management by objective has, in the main, been abandoned. Still, compared to the legacy he left, these are small gripes. He was the first and the greatest of the management thinkers and a genuine intellectual, who could have succeeded in any number of fields. In 1996, the *McKinsey Quarterly* wrote, 'Peter Drucker is the one Guru to whom other gurus kowtow.' This remains true. And as the *Economist* said in 2009, 'The most important reason why people continue to revere Drucker… is that his writing remains startlingly relevant.'

References and further reading

Beatty, Jack (2005) The education of Peter Drucker, *Atlantic*, December

Byrne, John A (2005) The man who invented management, *Businessweek*, 28 November

Caulkin, Simon (2005) Putting the man into manager, *Observer*, 20 November

Drucker School, Claremont Graduate University, Drucker biography and timeline, Claremont Graduate University website

Economist (2005) Remembering Drucker, 21 November

Economist (2005) Peter Drucker: trusting the teacher in the grey-flannel suit, 24 November

Economist (2009) Remembering Drucker, 19 November [Online] http://www.economist/node/14903040?story_id=14903040

http://www.druckersociety.at/index.php/peterdruckerhome/texts/friedrich-julius-stahl

Micklethwait, John and Wooldridge, Alan (1996) Drucker: the guru's guru, in *McKinsey Quarterly*, 22 June

Starbuck, Peter (2005) Obituary: Peter Drucker, *Guardian*, 14 November

Stern, Stefan (2009) Drucker's ideas stand the test of time, *Financial Times*, 24 November

Sullivan, Patricia (2005) Management visionary Peter Drucker dies, *Washington Post*, 12 November

Chapter Eleven
Ingvar Kamprad

Ingvar Kamprad's creation – the self-assembly furniture giant IKEA – is Sweden's best-known export. In fact, it's fair to say that, if you asked many people to name a Swedish company, IKEA is the only one they'd be able to come up with. As with so many of his fellow game changers, Kamprad's influence stretches far beyond mere commercial success, into our very culture and the way we live our lives. Indeed, IKEA has been the single greatest influence on how we furnish our homes in the last two decades – chances are you have an IKEA item in your house somewhere – and its effects are everywhere from the obvious to the obscure. At one end of the spectrum, the difficulty of assembling an IKEA item once home is a staple of stand-up comedy. And at the other the minimalist, modern aesthetic popularized by the company is largely credited with destroying the once-buoyant market for mid-range antiques in the UK. The man behind all this, Ingvar Kamprad, is an interesting mixture – he is extraordinarily frugal and a sometime alcoholic, had a youthful flirtation with Nazism, has an almost Calvinist work ethic and, perhaps above all, is the head of a company that can occasionally feel like a religious cult dedicated to the flat pack.

Ingvar Kamprad was born on 30 March 1926 in Småland in southern Sweden and grew up on a farm called Elmtaryd. According to the Kamprad legend, the young Ingvar, like teenagers the world over, was prone to laziness, and had a deep dislike of getting up to milk the cows in the morning; this pushed him to explore other ways of making a living. His earliest business venture involved selling matches. He realized that, if he bought them wholesale in Stockholm, he could sell them to his neighbours at a price that was considered cheap and still make a healthy profit. Soon he had diversified into pens, pencils, decorations and more. When Kamprad was 17, in 1943, his father gave him a sum of money as a reward for his school performance, and he used this to set up a business he called IKEA – the name comes from his initials, the name of the farm and the name of the local village, Agunnaryd; the company's early product line consisted of small consumer goods.

In 1946, Kamprad published his first newspaper ad (for ballpoint pens), and in 1948 he built his first warehouse, a shed on the family farm. Goods were delivered by milk truck. Furniture from local producers was introduced in 1948, and in 1951 the now iconic catalogue appeared. Then, as now, it cost customers nothing. The company opened a showroom in 1953, and in 1955 began to design its own furniture – this was in response to competitors pressurizing suppliers to boycott IKEA. A year later, the first flat-pack self-assembly item, the Lovet table, arrived. The concept of self-assembly was arrived at by accident – a worker removed the legs of the table in order to get it into a car without damage. In 1958, the first store opened in the town of Almhult – at 6,700 square metres, it was Sweden's largest furniture store. Two years later, the company opened its first in-store restaurant, serving its main non-furniture trademark – meatballs. In 1965, it opened a 31,000-square-metre store in Stockholm; soon there was a self-service warehouse.

Over the 1970s and 1980s the company expanded across Europe; in 1985, it opened its first store in Philadelphia; and in 1987 it was in the UK. The formula has been a resounding success – by 2008, the company had 253 directly controlled stores and over half a billion shoppers visited it during the year. Kamprad himself retired from management in 1986, to become an adviser to the company's parent group, INGKA Holdings, although as we shall see this is not quite retirement in the sense that most people mean it, and the degree of control Kamprad exercises over the company is still a matter of speculation. As the company's website rather elliptically notes, 'Ingvar Kamprad has never forsaken his "family". He works tirelessly as an advisor to senior management and continues to set a good example on his travels around the IKEA world by inspiring co-workers and enthusiastically proving that nothing is impossible. Ingvar Kamprad has never lost sight of his vision of creating a better everyday life for the many people.'

If this sounds quasi-religious to you then that's hardly surprising: many who have studied IKEA have noted that it feels halfway between a furniture store and a religion, with Kamprad as the high priest. He is famed for a work ethic that comes from growing up on a farm in a part of the world with poor, rocky soils, cold weather and long, dark winters. He is legendary for his frugality – he flies economy, he buys vegetables in the afternoon, as that's when they're cheapest, and he drives an old Volvo. He also wants his staff to do the same: employees are used as catalogue models, and managers are expected to share hotel rooms; he even expects staff to use both sides of a piece of paper. As he says, 'How the hell can I ask people who work for me to travel cheaply if I am travelling in luxury? It's a question of good leadership.' Now, well into his 80s, he still pays surprise visits to stores and hugs employees, in whom he often inspires devotion. You could argue that this view of self-reliance and thriftiness extends to his customers: IKEA stores are notorious as places where the customer does the work.

Kamprad himself does little to dispel the idea that IKEA has religious overtones. Normally, he is secretive and interview shy, and lives a reclusive life in Switzerland. When he does make formal pronouncements they are not what one would expect from a CEO. In a 1976 document entitled 'A furniture dealer's testament' he outlined his 'nine commandments', with the usual emphasis on thrift, self-reliance, humility, simplicity and the perpetuation of the 'IKEA spirit'. In 1999, with the Swedish journalist Bertil Torekull, he expanded these ideas in a book called *Leading by Design: The*

IKEA story, which was half-autobiography, half-corporate philosophy. In its review, the *Guardian* said:

> Kamprad's vision really is religious: the company exists to improve not just the lot of people, but the people themselves. Self-sufficiency is the watchword: you find your own way round the store, choose your goods with minimal assistance from staff, carry them to the check-out and the car, cart them home, and then assemble them yourselves. The company doesn't do this just because it keeps costs (and thus prices) down, but because it is good for you. It makes you a better person.

But this dedication to doing it yourself is why you can buy a coffee cup very cheaply, and you only have to look at IKEA's sales to see that most people are happier with paying less for less. The IKEA catalogue's print run, which is in the hundreds of millions, famously outstrips that of the Bible. The store is so popular that, at a UK opening in north London in 2005, five people were hospitalized in the stampede to get in; a year earlier, when a shop in Saudi Arabia offered $150 credit vouchers, three people were killed in the rush to get in. Of course, you do see similar consumer frenzies elsewhere – notably at the Apple stores, when another company that is sometimes compared to a cult launches new products. There have also been other modern furniture stores with a focus on design – such as the UK-based Habitat. But both Apple and Habitat produce expensive goods that make them a middle-class proposition, whereas IKEA really is for everyone; in fact, the company even sells flat-pack houses.

IKEA is not without its critics though. Some say the company's democratized version of style isn't really style at all and that the company offers the design equivalent of fast food. Writing in the *Times* (30 May 2010), the outspoken design critic Stephen Bayley said that 'Ikea has globalised a tacky version of the culture that fed it'; he has also described its design as mediocre. There are plenty of people who complain that IKEA has effectively extended the throwaway concept to furniture – when you move house, the thinking goes, it's not worth taking it with you and, even if you did, it probably wouldn't survive. Still on the design front, many hate its vast 'big-box' stores, which in their blue and yellow must count as some of the ugliest and least harmonious structures ever to sit in a landscape. Moreover, as an example of an out-of-town retailer, IKEA encourages car dependency and destroys small businesses according to critics.

There have been other allegations too. The company's supply chain has come under fire on several occasions, with accusers claiming that the ultimate price for cheap bookcases and tables is borne by the environment and citizens of the Third World; in 2009, the company was added to the Sweatshop Hall of Fame by the International Labor Rights Forum. The company has taken steps to address these issues, but many still say IKEA takes on board just as much criticism as it has to and that its lack of transparency makes it difficult to tell whether or not it's addressing the issues as it should.

The biggest criticisms of all though have been of the company's complicated ownership structure, which is the very definition of opaque. The IKEA group is owned by the Stichting INGKA Foundation, a Dutch charitable trust, which the *Economist* reckoned was worth $36 billion in 2006; this would make it the largest such trust in the world, bigger even than the Bill & Melinda Gates Foundation. However, its giving differs from the Gates Foundation's straightforward philanthropy in that the apparent grants that the Stichting INGKA Foundation makes are minuscule in comparison to its assets and income. Even more confusingly, the IKEA trademark and brand are owned by Inter IKEA Systems, which is a different Dutch company – and so it goes, all the way back via various holding companies to a trust in the Caribbean whose beneficiaries need not be disclosed. Unsurprisingly, IKEA refuses to comment on any of this. In 2006, the *Economist* wrote:

> What emerges is an outfit that ingeniously exploits the quirks of different jurisdictions to create a charity, dedicated to a somewhat banal cause [interior design], that is not only the world's richest foundation, but at the moment also one of its least generous. The overall set-up of IKEA minimises tax and disclosure, handsomely rewards the founding Kamprad family and makes IKEA immune to a takeover.

Kamprad said that one of the reasons he'd chosen not to float the company was that he didn't want to feel responsible to outsiders. He wasn't kidding.

There are other far more personal skeletons in his closet too. In 1994 a Swedish paper revealed that between the ages of 16 and 25 Kamprad had been involved in a Swedish far-right group and was friends with the movement's leader, Per Engdahl, a Nazi sympathizer – to the point of inviting him to his first wedding. Kamprad wrote to every employee explaining that he had made a youthful mistake, and the IKEA family forgave him. He has said, 'There are few people who have made so many fiascos in my life as I have.' Some have suggested that his economical man-of-the-people image may not be all it's cracked up to be either. He owns a vineyard and a mansion in Switzerland where he lives as a tax exile; indeed, for all the talk of Scandinavian thrift, IKEA long ago ceased to be a Swedish company. Perhaps the most extraordinary thing about this unusual man, though, is that he is a self-confessed alcoholic, albeit one who stops regularly to rest his liver and kidneys and claims to have his problem under control. He says: 'I dry out three times a year. My problem began when we visited Poland in the Sixties to buy materials. It was almost compulsory to take vodka with contacts.' He says he has no plans to give up drinking because 'it is one of life's treats'.

Still, compared to many of the cookie-cutter corporate brass of today, there is no doubt that Kamprad is fascinating – and there is also no doubt that most of his staff have a great deal of affection for him and the extraordinary company that he has built up. Quite what will happen when the man whose personality makes IKEA what it is dies remains to be seen. He's said that one of the reasons behind the complex ownership structure is to prevent family feuds: 'I've paid an awful lot of money to protect what I've built. I can only hope the money was well spent' (*Independent*, 23 July 2000).

References and further reading

Bailly, Olivier, Caudron, Jean-Marc and Lambert, Denis (2006) Low prices, high social costs: the sins of the founder found out, *Le Monde Diplomatique*, 1 December

BBC profile, Ingvar Kamprad

Crampton, Robert (2008) The home land: IKEA, *Times*, 7 June

Economist (2006) Ikea: flat packing, 13 May

Ellam, Dennis (2008) He is the world's 4th richest man, yet he drives an old Volvo, flies easyJet and at 81 is an alcoholic who dries out three times a year, *Sunday Mirror*, 13 April

Gold Coast Bulletin (2009) Man behind the flatpack, 13 June

Guardian (2004) Morality and meatballs, 17 June

Hagerty, James R (1999) How to assemble a retail success story, *Wall Street Journal*, 9 September

IKEA website, www.ikea.com

McLuckie, Kirsty (2008) Swede inspiration comes of age, *Scotsman*, 17 April

Swain, Gill (2005) The strange world of Mr Ikea, *Daily Express*, 12 February

Times (2005) Profile: Ingvar Kamprad, 13 February

Triggs, John (2003) Flat pack king who's given us Swede dreams, 26 August

Chapter Twelve
Oprah

Y ou have to start somewhere, and it may as well be with the talk show host, as that is the route Oprah Winfrey took to fame and fortune. But she is so much more than that. She is probably the most powerful woman in the United States and perhaps even the world. Her influence can shape elections in the world's most powerful country; her talk show is the highest rated and best known ever. She is a producer and a businesswoman who runs a huge empire. According to *Forbes*, she is the richest black person in the world – and she was at one point its only black billionaire. And yet, for all this, she is utterly accessible, has the common touch in abundance and is seen every day in millions of homes empathizing (often to the point of tears) with ordinary people.

Born in Mississippi in 1954, she was the daughter of a teenage single mother and a soldier and grew up in the kind of poverty and hardship that was common in the rural South at the time. Her parents split up shortly after she was born, and as a child she has said she wore dresses made from sacks and kept roaches as pets. She was clearly very bright, as she was taught to read by her grandmother before she was three. When she was six, her already straitened circumstances got far worse: she moved to inner-city Milwaukee. There she was raped by a cousin and an uncle, and she ran away from home at 13. At 14 she became pregnant, but the child died shortly after birth.

Perhaps surprisingly Winfrey's luck changed when she was sent to live with her father, Vernon Winfrey, who believed in education and discipline. At East Nashville High School she began to shine in a number of areas. She was an honours student, a talented orator and an accomplished actress. She won a scholarship to Tennessee State University and, aged 17, won a beauty pageant as Miss Fire Prevention. As a result of this she visited a local radio station and was offered a job reading the afternoon headlines. She clearly had the right stuff: at 19, she became the first black female newscaster in Nashville.

In 1976, she moved to Baltimore to host the six o'clock news. At first, this was something of a disaster. She was given an ill-advised makeover and was even asked to change her name to Suzy, which she refused to do. She wasn't the greatest TV journalist either – she found it hard to be objective and often became emotionally involved in the news she was meant to be reporting, crying at sad stories. Soon, she suffered a rare setback: she was demoted from news anchor to co-host of a morning talk show called *People Are Talking*, which was first aired in 1978. However, as we now know, this turned out to be a life-changing blessing in disguise. As she later said, she greatly preferred telling people's stories to reporting objective news: 'It was like breathing to me. Like breathing. You just talk.'

When it came to 'just talking', Winfrey clearly could do it. In 1983, she moved to Chicago to host the flagging *AM Chicago* programme. Soon it became the most watched talk show in the city, eclipsing Donahue's number one show, and was renamed *The Oprah Winfrey Show*. When the music guru Quincy Jones saw her he arranged for her to audition with Spielberg; the result was her playing the part of Sofia in *The Color Purple*, for which she was nominated for an Academy Award. In 1986, her show went national, and the success she had enjoyed in Chicago was repeated nationwide. An American icon had been created.

To understand why Oprah was such a success, it's necessary to remember that, back in the early 1980s, chat shows were very much a male preserve. Informality was creeping in; Donahue had pioneered the walking-and-talking-with-the-mike technique that broke down the physical barriers between host and audience, but it was Oprah who dismantled the emotional barriers. Although she's very intelligent in an academic sense, her emotional intelligence must be off the scale. She has a natural warmth, incredible empathy and an instinctive understanding of human nature – people just want to open up to her. Even though the show is broadcasting to a global audience of millions, the discussions between host and guest retain the intimate feel of two friends having a chat.

Moreover, Oprah wears her heart on her sleeve. Her revelations about herself have helped make it feel all the more real. With such a hard background she really can empathize with people who are going through terrible periods in their lives – there's nothing faked about it. Moreover, her frankness about her lifelong battle with her weight, which has been played out very visibly over the years, has endeared her greatly to her overwhelmingly female audience; the shame she feels over her yo-yoing weight is real. Indeed, a key 'Oprah moment' occurred in 1988 when she brought a child's wagon on to the stage with her, carrying 67 pounds of fat to demonstrate what she'd lost. She's got incredible drive too – and she needs it. With around 200 episodes a year, it's not as though she has a lot of time off, and that is before any of her numerous other business activities or appearances are taken into account.

It's perhaps worth noting here that, seven years after Oprah launched herself on the world, another hugely influential chat show, *The Jerry Springer Show*, also made its debut in Chicago. Indeed, for a while, the two appeared to be locked in a battle of the chat shows. In the 1990s, she said she deplored the vulgar direction chat shows were taking and that she wasn't going to try to 'out-Jerry Jerry'.

Oprah had business smarts as well as emotional nous though. Realizing that with her popularity came power, she decided to become the CEO of the product that was Oprah rather than simply being paid a very high wage. In 1986, she set up Harpo Productions (Harpo is Oprah spelt backwards) and took control of the show. The same year, the show was syndicated nationwide and earned $163 million. Her share of this was $39 million. She put this down to having a smart lawyer at the time, saying that she never thought such control was possible until he suggested it: 'Everyone needs someone in their life to say "yes, you can do it"' (*Australian Women's Weekly*, 2005). That smart lawyer, Jeff Jacobs, is still with her as President of Harpo – and is the little-seen business mind behind the brand.

Since then, Oprah's influence, reach and fortune have grown hugely, and there is no doubt that much of it has been for the good. Her book club is famous for persuading chat show viewers – who are not famous readers – to read, and many of her recommendations have been far from pulpy feel-good novels. When she recommended Toni Morrison's *Song of Solomon*, it sold more in three months than it had in 20 years. When the author James Frey's memoir *A Million Little Pieces* turned out to be as much a work of fiction as fact, Oprah's reaction and Frey's very public drubbing held the nation – even the world – transfixed. Indeed, such is the power of Oprah that even not appearing on her show can boost sales. Jonathan Franzen's *The Corrections* was selected to be a pick; then in an interview he expressed concern that being an Oprah pick would alienate male readers. His invite to appear was rescinded, and the surrounding hoo-ha drew a great deal of attention to the book, which went on to become a huge bestseller. At a later awards ceremony, Franzen thanked Oprah.

Oprah's greatest TV moments read like a litany of popular culture's greatest hits. When Michael Jackson agreed to a rare interview with her in 1993, it was one of the most watched television programmes ever made. In 2004, she famously gave a car away to every member of the studio audience – the cost of the cars was small change compared to the publicity it generated. In 2005, Tom Cruise memorably went nuts on Oprah, first jumping all over her couch and then declaring his undying love for Katie

Holmes. And, in 2010, when Sarah Ferguson disgraced herself in a newspaper sting, she sought out Oprah as a confessor and a redeemer.

It's not all trivia and *People* magazine froth though. She has tackled racism in the South. In 1993, she was instrumental in the passing of the National Child Protection Act, which advocated the establishment of a national database of convicted child abusers – when it was signed into law it was widely referred to as 'Oprah's Bill'. Her ability to gauge the national mood is outstanding. In the aftermath of Hurricane Katrina, she went straight down to New Orleans and listened to the survivors' stories – she empathized with them (for their present is her past) and entered the hell of the Superdome, demanding that something be done. Her reaction was contrasted very favourably with that of George W Bush, who managed little more than a fly-over.

She's more than just a mirror held up to the national mood too. She often swims against the tide, and to great effect. For instance, in a country where the Christian Right often seems to have a stranglehold on populist public discourse, she has long been a champion of gay rights. Perhaps her single most influential act ever, though, was in the political arena. She came out very early in support of Barack Obama – when her name was better known than his – and the Oprah effect is widely credited with being a key factor in his victory over Hillary Clinton in the primaries. Her supporting him was not without controversy or cost to her either – many of her female fans cried traitor when she endorsed him ahead of Clinton.

Interestingly, if there's one demographic that Oprah has struggled to reach, it's the male sex. The format and the content of her show are both famous for being something men don't really get. Long after she'd become an astonishing success, her profile among men remained low, and they tended to trivialize what she did. What eventually got the unfair sex to take her seriously was her enormous wealth – and her enormous ability to affect national events, up to and including presidential elections.

Along with her influence, the business has grown too. Her *O* magazine (she is on every cover) was the most successful magazine start-up ever and currently has a circulation of around 2.5 million; she owns a chunk of Oxygen Media, a cable company aimed at women; she makes a small fortune from speaking; and her website enjoys 70 million views a month. In 2008, she announced the Oprah Winfrey Network, a joint venture with the Discovery Channel. Underpinning all of this is the Oprah brand with its mix of empathy, personal growth and self-discovery. And it's a brand she protects religiously – whether it's refusing all requests to endorse products or making employees sign non-disclosure agreements. She has also kept Harpo almost entirely her own – she owns a little over 90 per cent, while Jacobs owns just under 10 per cent.

She is not without her detractors though, and criticisms of her have been largely par for the course. In terms of the media, there have been claims that she is responsible for dumbing down and has an obsession with banal weight-loss fads, touchy-feely twaddle and self-help gurus who are often little more than charlatans. Critics also say that she tends to pull her punches with celebrities and politicians she likes and that she is responsible for promoting and celebrating the kind of emotional incontinence typified by Princess Diana's death. Predictably there are also allegations that she's not quite the woman of the people she claims to be and has a taste for the high life.

In 2010 the biographer Kitty Kelley, the so-called 'First Lady of Scandal', released her Oprah biography. This contained a number of more substantive allegations; probably the most damning have concerned Oprah being cold and manipulative. But in the grand scheme of celebrity revelations, they are very small beer and are unlikely to do any real damage to the towering edifice that is brand Oprah. Moreover, it is an indication of the esteem in which Oprah is held that most of the United States' best-known talk shows turned down the opportunity to interview Kelley about the book. The writer herself was very candid about how the response was a sign of Oprah's power. She said: 'I don't think for a moment that Oprah got on the phone and said, "Barbara, don't have Kitty on. She doesn't have to. She is that powerful."'

Oprah recently announced what will be the biggest career change for her in decades. In 2009 she said that she would be ending the Oprah Winfrey Show in September 2011. This is probably a very smart move on her part, as although the show remains incredibly popular its ratings have slipped considerably in the 2000s, along with all of network TV's as the media have fragmented. In 2010, she announced that she would be hosting her own evening show, called *Oprah's Next Chapter*, on the Oprah Winfrey Network; this would be a huge boost for the Network. But some commentators have suggested that a career in politics might be a more suitable second act for a woman who is still only in her 50s. As Jon Friedman noted on the MarketWatch website, 'I suspect that Oprah has bigger dreams than simply making another billion bucks.'

References and further reading

Australian Women's Weekly (2005) A woman of substance: the story of Oprah, 9 February

Harris, Paul (2005) You go, girl, *Observer*, 20 November

Leonard, Tom (2010) The omnipotence of Oprah Winfrey, *Telegraph*, 13 April

Pearce, Garth (1999) When it's not so good to talk, *Sunday Times*, 7 February

Sellers, Patricia (2002) The business of being Oprah, *Fortune*, 1 April

Chapter Thirteen
Sam Walton

In terms of how a single retailer, in the form of Walmart, has affected US society, redrawn maps and changed the way people live, Sam Walton really has only Ray Kroc as a rival. In fact, the effects of the two – for good and for ill – are remarkably similar. Both are inextricably linked to the suburban, car-centred United States that grew up after the Second World War. Both have been enormously successful but have left many wondering about the price paid for that success by society as a whole. And both liked to portray themselves as common men, unaffected by their enormous wealth.

In the case of Walton, a cherished part of his 'Mister Sam' image was that, even when he was worth millions – and then billions – of dollars, he still drove a pick-up truck, which was said to smell strongly of his beloved dogs. Those who visited Walmart's headquarters would often find themselves picked up by its founder and owner – in this old and distinctly malodorous vehicle. When one of the dogs died in 1981, he wrote a loving tribute to the animal in the company magazine and named a line of dog food after him.

Sam Walton died in 1992 of blood cancer, aged 74, but the company that bears his name is a list of superlatives. It is the largest private employer in the United States, where it is also the largest company by revenue and the largest grocery seller; it is the largest retailer in the world. It is the largest employer in Mexico and one of the largest in Canada. It is also one of the most controversial companies in the world and has attracted considerable criticism for everything from its environmental record, to its treatment of employees, to its destruction of small-town economies.

As befits a US commercial giant, Sam Walton was a small-town boy. He was born in 1918, in Kingfisher, Oklahoma, and his parents moved to Missouri soon afterwards. A child of the Depression, he grew up in tough economic conditions, where his father often struggled to put food on the table – and young Sam was expected to do his bit. This was one of the keys to him. Walton was perhaps above all a very, very hard worker. He worked seven days a week, because that's what he loved to do. Famously, when dying from cancer, just weeks before the end, he had a local Walmart manager in for a hospital bed meeting about the store's sales figures. Many who knew him well said that for Walton work was leisure.

At school, he was not a particularly academic student, but he did work hard enough to get decent grades and was a good sportsman, shining at football and basketball. After graduating, he studied economics at the University of Missouri, where he delivered papers to fund his degree. It was at college that he learnt another great lesson: be a people person. Walton wanted to become the student body president – and his modus operandi was very simple. He spoke to everyone he saw before they spoke to him – and before long he was the best-known guy on campus and largely viewed favourably by his fellow students. At university he also developed a passion for learning, no matter what he was doing or where he was. He became a great believer in what management thinkers would later rename 'lifelong learning'.

Walton graduated with a BA in 1940, and went to work for JCPenney in Des Moines, Iowa. He has said that the way the company treated its employees (it took a deep interest in them, their opinions and their development) profoundly influenced his thinking.

He lasted there 18 months, leaving because the United States had entered the war and he had to return to Missouri to await induction into the Army. Between 1942 and 1945, he was a captain in the Army Intelligence Corps, stationed in the United States. He met and married his wife in 1943; they had four children.

After being discharged in 1945, Walton opened his first store in Newport, Arkansas. It was a Ben Franklin franchise, the kind of store known as five-and-dime (as the typical price point of its products was 5 and 10 cents). The company, which was possibly the United States' first franchisee business, took its name from the 18th-century statesman, scientist and popular thinker Benjamin Franklin, who coined the phrase 'A penny saved is a penny earned.' It still exists today, although it is a minnow compared to Walmart.

Walton opened his shop opposite a more established store and within a couple of years was doing more business than his competitor. In 1950, when his landlord failed to renew the lease, Walton upped sticks and moved the store to nearby Bentonville, Arkansas; he chose the town because he thought that it was a nice place and had potential for growth. It turned out he was right. Soon he had a number of stores in the area and all his children were working in them. Even in the 1950s, Walton was exhibiting the characteristics that would result in the biggest retailer in the world. He took a personal interest in his store managers and employees, who saw him as a very good boss. He had a simple, folksy set of business rules, and he wasn't afraid to experiment.

By 1960, Walton had over a dozen stores and was the biggest Ben Franklin franchisee in the United States. He was by this stage in his early 40s and doing very well. In fact, he had a career that would have satisfied many less driven men, but his world-changing business idea wouldn't come to him until he was well into his 40s. It wasn't quite the last roll of the dice that Ray Kroc's was, but equally Walton was showing all the signs of a man who was likely to do far better than many of his peers but who was unlikely to change the world.

The world of retail was changing very fast however. Up until the 1960s, the prevalent model for department stores and five-and-dimes was one with large numbers of shop assistants who served customers individually. Although many of the goods they sold were modern, the way that many stores actually functioned was something that the Victorians would have recognized. But in the eastern United States, which was very much the most modern part of the country, two trends were proving popular. One was self-service stores, and the other was discounting, the beginning of the 'pile it high, sell it cheap' philosophy. Walton travelled across the country to see how self-service worked and opened the first self-service shop, a Ben Franklin, in his area. Interestingly, although Walton was an early believer in self-service, he was always a huge champion of good service. One of his famous diktats, known as 'the 10-foot rule', is that you must say 'How may I help you?' to any customer who comes within 10 feet of you.

Walton was also very interested in discounting. This was already big in the metropolitan, developed east, and Walton firmly believed that it could work in smaller, rural markets such as his own. These areas had hitherto been ignored by larger retailers, who believed the rural populations were too small and too spread out to be worth bothering with. Walton, however, believed differently. He thought that, if he discounted enough, all these spread-out customers would find their way to him.

The trouble was that Ben Franklin's management didn't take the same view. Walton travelled to the company's Chicago headquarters to be told that they weren't interested. But, if his visit to the Windy City did little to persuade Franklin's top brass, it did a lot more to bolster Walton's belief that he was right. While in Chicago he visited one of the first Kmarts (another big US discount chain), and this convinced him that, even without Ben Franklin's support, discounting was the way to go. So, in 1962, when Walton was already in his mid-40s, the Walmart story proper finally began. He opened his first Walmart store in Rogers, Arkansas: Walton was finally on his way.

Walton was a great exponent of the 'Business is not rocket science' school of thinking. His famous 10 rules for building a business (see box) are mainly common sense. These were the template he followed. Over the next decade, he concentrated on the geographic area he knew and what he knew. Growth was deliberate, not particularly fast, and confined to Arkansas and the surrounding states; relationships and openness were stressed, and he knew all his store managers well. Walton famously preferred visiting stores to being stuck in head office and was more often than not to be found on the shop floor, asking staff how business was going. By 1969 he had 18 Walmarts and 14 Ben Franklin franchises.

Sam Walton's 10 rules for building a successful business

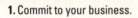

1. Commit to your business.

2. Share your profits with your people.

3. Motivate people to do their best.

4. Communicate what is going on.

5. Appreciate the people who are helping you.

6. Celebrate successes.

7. Listen to people when they speak, especially customers or clients.

8. Exceed expectations.

9. Control expenses better than your competition.

10. Swim upstream.

The company went public in 1971 and phased out the Ben Franklins. Of course, at this stage it was just another retail chain with little renown beyond its base. But Walton ploughed the money from the flotation back into the business – and worked with the extraordinary drive he'd always had. By 1977, he had 190 stores and, by 1985,

800. In 1985, his share of the company made him the richest man in the United States. In 1991, the company passed the retailer Sears in terms of size and opened its first store in Mexico; it now has nearly 1,500 units in the country.

Walton's great belief in lifelong learning never deserted him either. He was a passionate innovator whether it was the small (placing TV dinners next to diapers, as young couples with babies probably didn't have the time to cook) or being an early adopter of computer systems. He experimented with new types of stores, such as Sam's Club membership warehouses and Supercenters.

Walton was also a man who often saw around the next corner. While other retailers fought it out in metropolitan areas, he took the places that no one else wanted – but that were easy to drive to. In this sense, he might be seen as the father of out-of-town shopping. Like Ray Kroc, he scouted out new sites from the air, usually working out the best location for his new stores and then buying a parcel of land from the farmer in question.

Through all this, he remained folksy Sam – and he expected his staff to be like this too. All staff had plain offices that were lacking in ostentation to the point of being spartan, and this included top management. This, perhaps, is to be applauded. Other facets of the company culture are perhaps a little stranger. For starters there's the company 'Cheer':

> Give me a W!
> Give me an A!
> Give me an L!
> Give me a squiggly!
> Give me an M!
> Give me an A!
> Give me an R!
> Give me a T!
>
> What's that spell?
> Walmart!
>
> Whose Walmart is it?

107

It's my Walmart!

Who's number one?
The customer! Always!

'Don't be surprised if you hear our associates shouting this enthusiastically at your local Walmart store', warns the website. If this seems a little unsettling, there's plenty below the surface. The company's huge success has brought a lot of scrutiny, with plenty not liking what they see.

A piece in the *New York Times* in 2005 is fairly typical of the kind of charges levelled at Walmart by its detractors: 'An internal memo sent to Wal-Mart's board of directors proposes numerous ways to hold down spending on health care and other benefits while seeking to minimize damage to the retailer's reputation. Among the recommendations are hiring more part-time workers and discouraging unhealthy people from working at Wal-Mart.'

Moreover, while the company boasts of how cheap it is (for where else can you get a pair of Levi's for less than $20?) and aligns itself with hardworking families, others see it as a bully that abuses its suppliers, especially in low-wage economies. And if it's encouraging dubious labour practices abroad, at home it's everyone's favourite big-box villain, driving mom-and-pop stores out of business. When a Walmart opens, say critics, nearby town centres die and, although Walmart may portray itself as the friend of the average Joes with its low prices, it actually destroys local economies and impoverishes the average person. It is also pathologically anti-union. Indeed, according to critics, once you factor everything in, Walmart is actually exploiting the ordinary person – and the only US family who really benefit are the Waltons, who despite their cherished folksy image are among the richest people in the world.

Perhaps aware of a certain image problem that it has, Walmart has undertaken much of its international expansion under other names. In the UK, for instance, Walmart shoppers shop at Asda. Meanwhile, in 2006, the company withdrew from Germany at a cost of $1 billion, having pulled out of Korea earlier the same year. Commentators said that much of the reason was that the company's culture didn't travel well and that the liberal Germans found many of its highly conservative practices, especially in areas like labour, unacceptable.

But, whether or not Walmart can replicate its US success in the rest of the world, there is no doubt that Sam Walton's stores have been so influential that they have changed the human geography of a continent. It is also perhaps a mark of his success that his surviving children are all among the United States' top ten richest people. Only Bill Gates, Warren Buffett and Larry Ellison are richer.

References and further reading

Bell, John (1999) Sam Walton (1918–1992): everyday low prices pay off, *Journal of Business Strategy*, 1 September

Clark, Andrew (2010) Walmart, the US retailer taking over the world by stealth, *Guardian*, 13 January

Gross, Daniel (1996) *Forbes Greatest Business Stories of All Time*, pp 266–83

Hosenball, Mark (1985) Shy Sam, the man with billions in store, *Sunday Times*, 20 October

Markowitz, Arthur (1989) Mr Sam: Wal-Mart's patriarch, *Retailing Today*, 18 December

Meyerson, Howard (2009) In Wal-Mart's image, *American Prospect*, 1 September

Painter, Steve (2007) Friendly invasion: the annual shareholders meeting will bring hordes of national and international 'Wal-Martians' to Northwest Arkansas, *Arkansas Democrat-Gazette*, 20 May

Pilieci, Vito (2002) How Wal-Mart conquered the world, *Ottawa Citizen*, 2 April

Sunday Times (2001) Mr Sam – the folksy tycoon with a killer instinct, 10 June

Walmart, Samuel Moore Walton biography, walmartstores.com

Walton, Sam (1993) *Sam Walton: Made in America,* Bantam

Chapter Fourteen
Mary Kay Ash

When most people think of Mary Kay Ash, they probably think of cosmetics and little more. Those who remember her a little better might think of the colour pink, a penchant for a kind of Barbie bling and a taste in interiors that was modelled on the taste of her close friend Liberace. Those who actually worked for and with her knew that she was far more than that – and beneath all that candy floss-coloured extroversion was a highly principled, determined and successful businesswoman whose ideas were often years, if not decades, ahead of her time.

Ash was a hugely rich and successful businesswoman in a world that was, by today's standards, astonishingly sexist. Because she'd been on the receiving end of gender discrimination so many times, when she finally set up on her own her ideas about management were pretty radical. Some of them seemed downright eccentric at the time, but if you look at them closely you see the ideas of a woman who genuinely knew how to engage and motivate people, who promoted according to ability rather than gender and who worried about her staff's work–life balance decades before the term even existed. Indeed, although the two were superficially quite different, there are plenty of interesting parallels between Ash and that other female cosmetics Titan, Anita Roddick.

Mary Kay was also interesting in her celebrity status and how she used it. She worked in an era when businesspeople (the vast majority of whom were men) did not as a rule court attention and play up their roles. As with many of her ideas, her profile and how she used it seem more in tune with the early 21st century than the mid-20th. As an iconoclast, she had fans ranging from Laura Bush, to *Fried Green Tomatoes* author Fannie Flagg, to members of the Dallas Cowboys football team. Lest you think she was a triumph of style over substance, her staff genuinely loved her: when she died, employees past and present queued up to offer often tearful tributes. They praised her unselfishness and told of how she'd changed their lives. For many, it was as though a family member had died. A typical eulogy began, 'We all loved her...'

Mary Kay was born Mary Kathryn Wagner, in 1918, in Hot Wells, Texas, a rural spa town that is now being swallowed up by Houston's urban sprawl; her parents operated a popular hotel and restaurant. When Ash was seven, her father contracted tuberculosis and had to move into a sanatorium. Her mother sold the businesses, and the family moved to Houston. Her mother worked 14-hour shifts in a restaurant, and Ash helped out around the house with cooking and cleaning. Despite their reduced circumstances, her mother was inspirational to Mary Kay: even with her long hours, she found time to encourage her daughter, constantly telling her that she could do anything she put her mind to. Ash often cited this as the wellspring of her self-confidence: 'My mother's words became the theme of my childhood. They have stayed with me all my life.'

Ash was a good student, but her straitened circumstances precluded college and, in 1935, she married Ben Rogers, who worked at a gas station, sang in a local band and did radio work. The couple went on to have three children, but the marriage did not last. Ash wrote that it collapsed after Rogers joined the Army. They divorced when he returned from the Second World War; she said that this was the lowest point of her life and that 'I felt like a complete failure as a woman'. Moreover, she had three children to provide for by herself.

Ash started studying medicine at the University of Houston. She also worked as a secretary and took a part-time job with Stanley Home Products (SHP), which sold household goods such as brooms and toothbrushes; the company is said to have originated party sales (as in, most famously, the Tupperware party). Ash attended an SHP convention in Dallas, which changed her life. There, the company crowned a Sales Queen – and Ash suddenly had a goal. The following year, Ash was the Sales Queen, but she went on to become so successful she unnerved SHP's board, who moved her to Dallas and clipped her wings.

In 1952, she left for another direct sales company, World Gifts. The pattern repeated itself: in her first year she was earning over $1,000 a month, equivalent to about $8,000 now and over four times the national average. But the pattern of discrimination she'd seen at SHP repeated itself. Ash was at World Gifts for 11 years and eventually left for a combination of reasons. One of them was that she wanted to write a book for women in business based on her experiences. Another was that she was tired of being passed over in favour of less well-qualified male colleagues. The company's website states that the final straw was when a man who had been hired as her assistant and trained by her was promoted over her at twice her salary. Ash would later say:

> I learned back then that as long as men didn't believe women could do anything, women were never going to have a chance. I knew that I had been denied opportunities to fulfil my optimum potential simply because I was a woman. These feelings were not mere indulgences of self-pity, because I had personally known so many other women who had suffered similar injustices.

Although Ash had intended to write a book, things turned out very differently. The ideas she'd been mulling over for her various chapters were to become her company instead. She is said to have sat down at her kitchen table and written two lists: one was the good things she'd seen at companies; the other was areas that she believed could be improved. When she looked over the two, something clicked. This wasn't a book; it was a business plan. So, in 1963, with her $5,000 life savings and the help of her son Richard, she opened Beauty by Mary Kay in a 500-square-foot shop in Dallas. The furniture was second-hand and the curtains were handmade, but she was on her way. The company's core product was a skin cream to which she had bought the manufacturing rights. This is supposed to have been developed by a hide tanner whose daughter had noticed that his skin was far younger than one would expect. Her consultants were independent: they bought wholesale and sold retail but were essentially running their own business.

It's perhaps worth remembering here that, in common with quite a few mid-20th-century business game changers such as Ray Kroc and Sam Walton, Mary Kay was no spring chicken when she founded her business; in fact she was already 45. Later, in response to being asked how she succeeded so quickly, she said, 'The answer is I was middle aged, had varicose veins and I didn't have time to fool around.' Of course, this might have given her the push she needed, but the real reason might have been seeing how businesses treated talented women.

She also said, 'I wasn't that interested in the dollars and cents part of the business. My interest in starting Mary Kay was to offer women opportunities that didn't exist anywhere else.' It doesn't take a genius to work out that one of the greatest ways to motivate people is to offer them the opportunities they have been denied to them everywhere else. In her motivation speeches at company get-togethers Ash would often say, 'I want you to become the highest-paid women in America.' Quite a few of those who worked for her took this advice to heart: by the time she died, 150 women had earned more than $1 million working for her.

With her own company, Ash left her years of struggle behind her. The company started out with 11 beauty consultants and did nearly $200,000 in sales in its first year. The following year, it quadrupled this to $800,000. In 1964, she began a tradition – the company seminar. The first was essentially a big get-together over dinner, with Mary Kay cooking chicken and making jello salad for the company's 200 staff and consultants. It was held in a warehouse decorated with balloons and crêpe paper; she even served it herself on paper plates. This meal was the first of the company's famous seminars and, as her cosmetics empire grew, these would become ever more lavish events that often felt more like showbiz parties than corporate AGMs. Yet these events served a serious function. The company offered motivational courses and training, and there were the awards where the company's stars received honours and prizes worth tens of thousands of dollars. In 2009, 35,000 people attended. Most of them were the company's consultants, who as they effectively run their own businesses have to pay their own travel and accommodation costs.

Ash's Dallas seminars (they are now held in countries all over the world) became legendary. Her paying attendees even included professors from Harvard Business School who could see that below all the pink and diamonds was a business brain that genuinely did think differently.

In 1968, she bought her first Cadillac, which she had repainted pink to match one of her products. The car was such a hit (and a good marketing device) that she gave similar cars to her top five consultants. The company now offers a broad range of cars (not all of which are pink). As of 2006, GM estimated that it had produced 100,000 pink Cadillacs for Mary Kay. As she said, 'Recognition is the key.'

During the 1970s, the company boomed. By the end of the decade it had sales of over $100 million and a listing on the New York Stock Exchange. With her distinctive appearance and flamboyance, Ash had become a kind of celebrity. She has been referenced hundreds of times in popular culture and had to leave many of her public appearances like a rock star through back doors and tunnels to avoid being mobbed by her adoring fans.

Yet, despite all this, her (and her company's) philosophy remained much as it always had been. She believed in treating others as you would want to be treated yourself (staff and consultants were encouraged to behave as if everyone they met had a sign around their neck saying 'Make me feel important'). She was a keen believer in work–life balance or, as this was Texas, work–life–faith balance: staff were told to put God first, family second and career third. (This makes for an amusing contrast with Ray Kroc's diktat. He said: 'I believe in God, family and McDonald's – and in the office that order is reversed.') Finally, she believed that anyone could succeed, given the right encouragement. Occasionally her star performers and recipients of pink Caddies were even men.

In the mid-1980s, though, the company faltered. Sales and the share price dropped, and in 1985 the family took the company private again in a $450 million leveraged buyout. Ash retired in 1987. She had a stroke in 1996, and afterwards her health was poor. She died in 2001, aged 83; that year the company's sales were over $1 billion. In 2010, they were closer to $3 billion. Over the years Ash had received dozens of business awards and was widely liked and admired. In an arena where many are highly controversial, few had anything bad to say about her. But this is hardly surprising given that her motives were by and large very good.

In her *New York Times* obituary she is quoted as telling a friend:

> In 1963, the social forces that now support the financial and legal equality of women had not gained public favour. And yet here was a company that would give women all the opportunities I had never had. I don't think God wanted a world in which a woman would have to work 14 hours a day to support her family, as my mother had done. I believe he used this company as a vehicle to give women a chance.

References and further reading

AP/*Houston Chronicle* (2010) Mary Kay Ash, cosmetics giant dead at age 83, 23 November

AP/*St Louis Post-Dispatch*, Cosmetics empire was started to offer women opportunities; company grew from sales force of 11 to 750,000 in 37 countries

Bodor, Jim, 'We all loved her': local associates recall legacy of Mary Kay Ash, *Telegram & Gazette*, Worcester, MA

Dallas Morning News
Detroit Free Press (2001) Obituary, 23 November
Gross, Daniel (1996) *Forbes Greatest Business Stories of All Time*, pp 232–45
Mary Kay tribute website, marykaytribute.com
Mary Kay website, biography, www.marykay.com
Nemy, Enid (2001) Mary Kay Ash, builder of a beauty empire, dies at 83, *New York Times*, 24 November

Chapter Fifteen
Bill Gates

Bill Gates is one of the great drivers of the information revolution of the late 20th century and has done more to shape the personal computer experience than any other person. In 1975, he memorably described a future computer in every home and on every desk and, to a great extent, this vision has come true, largely because of his efforts. The company he founded, Microsoft (MS), makes the Windows operating system that powers over 90 per cent of the world's PCs, while its Office productivity suite is thought to be used by something like 80 per cent of the world's enterprises. Much of what we take for granted in the world of computing – from document standards to buzzwords – has had its genesis at Microsoft.

All this made Gates the world's richest man for an extraordinarily long time – he held the title from 1993 to 2007. Indeed, at one point Gates was so wealthy he was worth over $100 billion, a figure that eclipsed the GDP of most of the world's countries. The reason he no longer holds the number one spot is because he has given so much of his fortune to charity. Even so, despite having given $20 billion to charity (second only to Warren Buffett), he is still the world's second-richest man, eclipsed only by the Mexican telecoms tycoon Carlos Slim Helú – and even then not by much. Naturally Gates has the ear of global leaders, he is routinely ranked as one of the world's most powerful men, and now, thanks to the Bill & Melinda Gates Foundation, he is the world's most important philanthropist.

Perhaps strangely given his generosity, neither Gates nor his company enjoys anything like the public affection that his two biggest rivals, Apple and Google, bask in. In fact, while people in the tech community eagerly await Apple and Google's every offering, with MS the relationship is more love to hate than love. Geeks seem to go out of their way to disparage MS products; they want to find things wrong with them. The company, the usual line of criticism goes, is anti-competitive. Its monopolistic practices allow it to offer expensive, overpriced and not terribly good software that businesses and consumers have no choice but to buy as well over 90 per cent of computers run on MS operating systems. When real alternatives appear, according to this line of thought, MS crushes them. Nor is it just consumers. Microsoft has attracted plenty of criticism – and the attention of quite a few governments – usually because it is seen as anti-competitive and monopolistic.

While people rarely hate Gates himself, there's no doubt that the spark that makes a Steve Jobs (or a Richard Branson) is lacking in Bill. He's rich, but he's not charismatic. Nevertheless, whatever people think about MS, they still buy its products, and it remains a huge and hugely powerful (if not hugely loved) force in the world of technology and business.

Gates was born in 1955, in Seattle, Washington, to wealthy parents. He had a comfortable upbringing; his father was a wealthy lawyer, while his mother was influential in the non-profit organization the United Way. It was thought that William H Gates III might follow in his father's footsteps. Gates showed early signs of brilliance, and his parents sent him to the expensive private Lakeside School. At the school, he met Paul Allen, who was two years older, and the two became fascinated by the school's Teletype machine, an early and very primitive computer. By the age of 17 Gates had sold his first piece of software (a timetabling program for his school) to the school and been paid $4,200 for it.

His early academic prowess was a taste of things to come. He scored 1590 (out of a possible 1600) on his SATs and went to Harvard. There, he became friends with Steve Ballmer, a fellow student who, years later, would succeed him as CEO of Microsoft. In late 1974, Allen, who had dropped out of university and was a programmer for Honeywell in Boston, read a piece in the magazine *Popular Electronics* about a microcomputer called the Altair, one of the world's first. Priced at $350, it was within the reach of ordinary people. The computer's makers, a New Mexico-based company called MITS, were inviting *Popular Electronics*'s readers to devise a programming language for it. Gates and Allen called MITS to say they'd developed a version of BASIC (the beginner-friendly programming language). They hadn't, but the company expressed interest, so the pair pulled out all the stops and made their claim come true. When Allen demonstrated their software to MITS in New Mexico, the company was so pleased it made him a vice president.

Here Gates took time out from Harvard to join Allen in New Mexico, and the pair began to call their own venture Micro-Soft. Gates then returned to Harvard briefly, but had dropped out altogether by late 1976. That year, they registered the trademark Microsoft, became independent of MITS and started taking on staff. By the end of 1978, the company's revenues were over $1 million. In early 1979, they moved the company to Washington near their home town, and in 1980 Steve Ballmer was taken on as business manager.

In 1980, Gates was asked by IBM to provide a BASIC interpreter for its upcoming computer, the IBM PC, which is the grandfather of virtually every mainstream computer in use today. IBM also needed an operating system and, after its discussions with another company failed, Microsoft agreed to provide it. For this, Microsoft licensed an operating system called 86-DOS, which had been written by Tim Paterson of Seattle Computer Products; for use in IBMs it was renamed PC-DOS. Microsoft would later buy it outright. This was where MS was very smart and completely outflanked IBM. Indeed, the deal that MS struck would turn out disastrously for the larger company and would ultimately result in one of the great shifts of power in the sector – from hardware makers to software makers. Indeed, you could argue that it was simply one of the great industrial shifts.

MS believed that it was very likely that other companies would clone IBM's hardware, so it retained the rights to license the operating system to non-IBM manufacturers; it's probably worth noting here that, while MS were very smart in the deal, IBM sleepwalked into it. The result (when the expected cloning did happen) was that Microsoft had a huge ready-made market for its operating system, while IBM was left making hardware, which was rapidly becoming a low-margin commodity.

In 1981, the company incorporated: Gates got 53 per cent, Allen 31 per cent and Ballmer 8 per cent; its revenues were $16 million, and it had 128 employees. Two years later, in 1983, these figures had tripled. But 1983 had a low point too. Allen was diagnosed with Hodgkin's disease. He was treated successfully, but he left Microsoft and thereafter pursued a career largely separate to MS, despite his vast holdings.

If DOS had given MS huge clout and resources, the software that was to make it a household name was just around the corner. In 1985, MS released a graphical interface for MS-DOS; this was Windows 1.0. The following year, the company went public. Its shares, which were priced at $21, shot up $7 on the first day's trading. Since then, they've split nine times, and the initial $21 would be worth over $7,000 in 2010. In 1987, Windows 2 appeared (Windows 3 and 4 followed), and in 1989 Office made its debut. Meanwhile, in another foretaste of things to come, Apple sued MS, claiming that Windows infringed its graphical user interface (GUI); Apple lost after six years.

The early 1990s saw MS at the very height of its powers. Its fortunes continued to wax, and the huge growth in computing, both in the home and in business, drove its revenues and profits ever higher. In 1992, *Forbes* anointed Gates the richest man in the United States, and the following year MS overtook IBM in terms of market capitalization, marking the end of an era. In 1994, Gates married his long-term girlfriend, Melinda French, and they subsequently had three children. In 1995, to huge fanfare, Windows 95, the first recognizably modern Windows, was launched. It was a stunning success and by almost any measure was one of the greatest product launches ever.

Yet, although MS was at its zenith, the forces that would later cause it so much trouble had been stirring since the early 1990s. The company had already attracted the interest of the US Justice Department, which was concerned that it was violating antitrust rules. Perhaps even more importantly, something called the internet was creating a huge buzz in technology and business circles. Bill Gates wasn't very interested – or at least not at first. Then in 1994 the company Netscape launched its famous Mosaic Navigator, and the net started to look like something ordinary people might like and businesses might use. In another foretaste of things to come, Netscape was giving its software away free. For the first time ever, it seemed faintly possible that history might repeat itself and someone else might do to MS what MS had done to IBM.

Gates changed his position quickly. In 1995, in a famous memo, he announced that the internet was in fact of the 'highest level of importance'; later in that year he would announce MS's own browser, Internet Explorer. This finally appeared in August 1996. It's worth remembering that by this stage Amazon had already been trading for a year. This perhaps marked the point where Microsoft ceased to be the only voice that really counted in computing. For the first time in years, the agenda was being set by others.

The company response did little to enhance public perceptions either. Netscape later claimed that Microsoft used its monopoly position to bully and cajole Windows users into ditching Netscape in favour of Explorer (which eventually led to Netscape losing most of its market and being bought out). In 1996 Netscape asked the US Department of Justice to investigate MS for anti-competitive practices. Two years later the Department of Justice and 20 state attorney generals sued MS. In 1998 Gates memorably gave a video deposition to the Department of Justice. This was widely viewed as evasive, rather dishonest and not terribly helpful. Microsoft lost, and the judge ordered it be broken up. In fact, the final settlement was far less draconian, and many regarded it as a mere slap on the wrist. But it did little for Microsoft or Gate's image. The former was widely characterized as an abusive monopolist and the latter as a control freak.

But 2000 saw the start of Gates's next chapter when he began to relinquish control of his empire: Ballmer became CEO, with day-to-day responsibility for running the company, and Gates became Executive Chairman. In 2001, the company launched Windows XP, which, after a few teething troubles, was widely praised; indeed it is still offered today and until very recently was seen as the operating system of choice for smaller, less powerful laptops.

Overall, the 2000s have not been kind to Microsoft, although, as the two have slowly begun to drift apart, they have perhaps been kinder to Bill Gates. Microsoft's rival Apple, which had a pretty awful decade in the 1990s, was having a far better time in the 2000s and, with Steve Jobs again at the helm, was starting to set the agenda. In 2001, Apple launched the iPod and in 2007 the radical iPhone. Both were game changers and also harbingers of the digital world of the future. MS, by comparison, had its unloved smartphones and its unremarked-upon Zune.

Meanwhile, in the late 1990s, Google had appeared and, although it didn't seem a threat at first, it soon would. Over the past decade it has sometimes seemed that Google's job is to make Microsoft's forays into the online arena look bad. If you take everything from Hotmail and Gmail to Microsoft Virtual Earth (now Bing Maps) and Google Earth, it's hard to escape the conclusion that, if it's online, Google does it better. Rather unfairly, this seems to work whether Google does it first (like Google Earth) or second (like Gmail). In the way that the early 1990s had seen power shift from equipment makers to software producers, it now seemed that all the excitement had gone online and into shiny gadgets, neither of which was really MS's area.

It gets worse too. Many believe that smartphones are where all the growth is in terms of internet access, and the ones to bet on are the iPhone and phones running Android – a free, open-source, Linux-based operating system that was developed by arch-rival Google. Worse still, these operating systems may be creeping out of the phone arena. iPad-type computers are looking very popular – and they're not looking like Windows machines. Rather they're either made by Apple or using Android. The worry for MS is that they could be the thin end of the wedge. The other great worry is that the functionality in many applications (such as those in Office) is migrating online, where the advantage is Google's. It sometimes looks as though MS is beset on all sides.

The company has had other troubles too. It's first big operating system launch of the 2000s, Windows Vista, which launched in 2007, was widely criticized and never caught on in the way that XP had. In 2008, the EU fined MS 899 million euros for failing to comply with antitrust rulings, and it failed to win its bid for Yahoo after the two companies failed to agree on a price. Worse still, arch-rival Apple recently overtook Microsoft in size.

But despite all these portents of doom and gloom, predictions of MS's downfall are greatly overstated. For one thing, it's very unlikely that people are going to stop buying Windows-based computers for a while yet. Moreover, MS's new operating system, Windows 7, has been widely regarded and remedies many of the faults of Vista. It's worth remembering, too, that it's always tempting to bash the incumbent. Perhaps the time that MS really needs to worry is when people are no longer complaining about it. The company remains a giant, if one that perhaps needs to be a little more agile.

Perhaps the biggest surprise for Gates's critics though was what he was starting to do with all that money. In the late 1990s, he started making multibillion-dollar donations to the Bill & Melinda Gates Foundation, a charity set up by him and his wife that concentrates on health and education. In 2006, Gates announced that he would be stepping back from MS to concentrate on his philanthropy, effective from mid-2008. He remains Microsoft's Chairman – and his holdings are still considerable – but he is now a philanthropist rather than a businessman. He's clearly an effective one too: in 2006, his friend Warren Buffett announced he would be giving away around $40 billion – and most of it would go to the Bill & Melinda Gates Foundation.

References and further reading

Bank, David (1999) Breaking windows, *Wall Street Journal*, 2 January

Bill & Melinda Gates Foundation website, www.gatesfoundation.org

Bolger, Joe (2006) I wish I wasn't the richest man in the world, says Bill Gates, *Times*, 5 May

Gates, Bill (1995) *The Road Ahead*

Gates, Bill (1999) *Business at the Speed of Thought*

Gross, Daniel (1996) 7 *Greatest Business Stories of All Time*, pp 334–51

Heilemann, John (2000) The truth, the whole truth, and nothing but the truth, *Wired*, 46

Microsoft website, www.microsoft.com

Smoking Gun, Mug shots

Wasserman, Elizabeth (1998) Gates deposition makes judge laugh in court, *CNN.com*, 17 November

Chapter Sixteen
David Ogilvy

For those who are interested, the very first thing that David Ogilvy wrote in a professional capacity is still available on the web. It goes by the rather recondite title 'The theory and practice of selling the Aga cooker' and was written in 1935, when he was in his mid-20s and working as a salesman for the UK's iconic cooker company. Of course, given its vintage, it's full of retrospectively amusing sexist howlers. But even so, it's a clear, persuasive and compelling read, 75 years on, with memorable lines such as 'The good salesman combines the tenacity of a bulldog with the manners of a spaniel.' *Fortune* magazine once called it 'the best sales manual ever written'.

Much of modern advertising owes its existence to David Ogilvy and his ideas. Many iconic mascots, slogans and brand identities owe their existence to Ogilvy and the agency he founded. Yet in many ways he was far from a typical ad man. In an industry famed for its ruthlessness and cynicism, he was anything but. In fact, if anything, his greatest single insight was nothing more than that consumers might actually be intelligent and shouldn't be treated as idiots. He disdained the idea of advertising as some sort of creative art and was frank about its job as selling. (He said, 'If it doesn't sell, it isn't creative' and 'I do not regard advertising as entertainment or an art form, but as a medium of information.') Yet his ads were about ideas, he wrote untold reams of copy (and never quite got on with television) and he was educated, deeply cultured and immensely witty. Indeed, he could barely open his mouth without *bons mots* dropping out.

One of his most famous quotes (and he was immensely quotable) is 'The consumer is not a moron, she is your wife.' Other great diktats included 'Never run an advertisement you wouldn't want your family to see' and 'Tell the truth but make it fascinating.' He also famously used the products he advertised whether they were Rolls-Royces or shirts. He described this as 'elementary good manners'. He even resigned accounts when he felt he could no longer believe in the product.

David Ogilvy was born in West Horsley, not far from London, in 1911. His father was a stockbroker, whose business had been badly affected by the economic downturn of the 1920s. As a result, his upbringing is probably best characterized as one of genteel poverty. He attended St Cyprian's School, Eastbourne, on reduced fees, before winning a scholarship to Fettes College, Edinburgh (the same school that Tony Blair attended), at 13. Afterwards, he won a scholarship to Oxford to study history at Christ Church in 1929. However, student life didn't agree with him. He described himself as a 'dud' and was eventually sent down for laziness; he later described this as 'the real failure of my life'. In 1931, he moved to Paris, where he got a job at the Hotel Majestic. This lasted a year; he said that it taught him discipline and management – and when to move on. 'If I had stayed at the Majestic I would have faced years of slave wages, fiendish pressure and perpetual exhaustion.'

So Ogilvy returned to England, where he began selling the Aga cooker door to door. He was, by all accounts, an outstanding salesman. This was noticed at Aga headquarters, and he was asked to write an instruction manual for other salesmen in 1935. His brother, who worked in advertising for the firm Mather & Crowther, read the manual and was impressed. This was Ogilvy's first big break. Ogilvy's brother showed it to his colleagues, with the result that Ogilvy was offered the position of Account Executive. Ogilvy showed an early flash of genius when he was given only $500 to advertise a newly opened hotel. Even in the 1930s, this was a derisory amount. He spent it on postcards and then sent them to everyone in the area phone book; the hotel opened full. After his method succeeded he wrote that 'I have tasted blood.' It gave him a lifelong belief in direct marketing, which has always been seen as advertising's poor and slightly disreputable relation.

Three years later, he managed to convince the agency to send him to the United States for a year. He was a hit with Americans (back then a British accent really did open doors) and became fascinated by the country. At the end of the year he resigned from Mather & Crowther and joined George Gallup's national research institute. His job for Gallup was gauging the popularity of Hollywood movie stars and stories for the studios. This work gave him an opportunity to travel widely in the United States and learn a great deal about it and also taught him the value of understanding what ordinary people thought.

During the Second World War, he worked in intelligence at the British Embassy in Washington. Although this work involved being trained as a spy, what he wound up doing was more humdrum – report writing and analysis. During this time he tried to bring his knowledge of behaviour to matters military and diplomatic. His reports were well received. After the war Ogilvy made another change in direction. He bought a farm in rural Lancaster County, Pennsylvania, which is famous for its Amish population. There, he farmed for several years, growing tobacco, although eventually he recognized that he was never going to make a success of farming, much as he loved the area and some aspects of the lifestyle.

In 1948, he was ready to found his own agency. He called it Hewitt, Ogilvy, Benson & Mather and did it with the backing of Mather & Crowther in London. At the time, he had $6,000 in the bank and was 38 years old. Despite his time in advertising and with Gallup, his CV really was pretty thin. He memorably noted afterwards that, at this point, he had never actually written an advertisement in his life. Indeed, by the time most people are well on their way up the ladder, Ogilvy had an eclectic smattering of experience in disparate (and mostly irrelevant) fields, had no degree and was unemployed.

However, he did have a feel for advertising, and the new company's ads were soon huge hits. Ogilvy memorably told us that Dove soap was a quarter moisturizing cream, and Dove went on to become the biggest brand in its sector. He invented the man in the Hathaway shirt, an aristocrat who had lost an eye and had to wear a patch. The patch instantly made a fairly nondescript middle-aged man in a shirt an object of mystery and intrigue. Ogilvy's copy at the bottom helped, of course, for he had a wonderful if rather strange way with words. The copy famously began 'The melancholy disciples of Thorstein Veblen would have despised this shirt.' Veblen was a sociologist and the author of *The Leisure Class*. It's doubtful whether even 1 per cent of people who saw the ad knew this, but it was a great and intriguing story, and an icon was born. Hathaway's sales shot up, and the company became a major brand. Ogilvy later wrote that the success of his one-eyed aristocrat baffled even him: 'Exactly why it turned out to be so successful, I shall never know. It put Hathaway on the map after 116 years of relative obscurity.'

He memorably had a stab at rebranding Puerto Rico as a cultural destination, saying 'Pablo Casals is coming home to Puerto Rico.' It worked. The company's Schweppes ads that featured a cultured Brit coming to the United States offering Schweppervescence ran for an extraordinary 18 years. As Ogilvy once said, 'every advertisement must contribute to the complex symbol which is the brand image'. He was a man of great charm. In the early 1960s *Time* magazine reported that he'd been given an account to sell the United States as a tourist destination to various West European countries, 'Every advertisement I write for the US travel service', Ogilvy quipped, 'is a bread and butter letter from a grateful immigrant.'

In 1959, the agency won the Rolls-Royce account. This campaign was one of his favourites. It read, 'At 60 miles per hour the loudest noise in this new Rolls-Royce comes from the electric clock.' It was a great success. Over its first 20 years, and from a standing start, the agency won prestige accounts such as Lever Brothers, General Foods, American Express, Shell and Sears. Indeed, if Ogilvy had a flaw, it might have been a tendency to oversell himself. He wrote of this time, 'I doubt whether any copywriter has ever had so many winners in such a short period of time', adding that the agency was 'so hot that getting clients was like shooting fish in a barrel'.

Perhaps because of his vanity, some said that his greatest creation was himself. Still, as they say, he had a great deal to be immodest about. He was a great writer, with a quick wit, who combined British manners, accent and eccentricity with American hard work and a distaste for the self-love of his industry. Physically he was striking – tall and red-haired – and he dressed stylishly and smoked a pipe. Set against all this, was a rather large ego so bad? In the early 1960s Ogilvy decided to write a book. It was intended to be a how-to manual for those entering the industry. With an ear for a snappy title he called it *Confessions of an Advertising Man*. With its crisp prose and catchy name, the book reached an audience far beyond Madison Avenue. The initial print run was 5,000, but to date it has sold over a million copies and is still considered required reading in the industry. He went on to write two other books.

David Ogilvy quotes

- 'A good advertisement is one which sells the product without drawing attention to itself.'

- 'Don't bunt. Aim out of the ball park. Aim for the company of immortals.'

- 'First, make yourself a reputation for being a creative genius. Second, surround yourself with partners who are better than you are. Third, leave them to go get on with it.'

- 'If you ever have the good fortune to create a great advertising campaign, you will soon see another agency steal it. This is irritating, but don't let it worry you; nobody has ever built a brand by imitating somebody else's advertising.'

- 'It strikes me as bad manners for a magazine to accept one of my advertisements and then attack it editorially – like inviting a man to dinner then spitting in his eye.'

- 'Many people – and I think I am one of them – are more productive when they've had a little to drink. I find if I drink two or three brandies, I'm far better able to write.'

- 'Ninety-nine per cent of advertising doesn't sell much of anything.'

Thirty-three years after founding his agency he wrote the following memo to another director:

Will Any Agency Hire This Man? He is 38, and unemployed. He dropped out of college. He has been a cook, a salesman, a diplomatist and a farmer. He knows nothing about marketing and had never written any copy. He professes to be interested in advertising as a career (at the age of 38!) and is ready to go to work for $5,000 a year. I doubt if any American agency will hire him. However, a London agency did hire him. Three years later he became the most famous copywriter in the world, and in due course built the tenth biggest agency in the world. The moral: it sometimes pays an agency to be imaginative and unorthodox in hiring.

As Stephen Bayley (2009) wrote in the *New Statesman*, 'Ogilvy's psychology was complicated. He knew Shakespeare and wrote beautifully, but wanted to be seen only as an evolved version of the doorstepping salesman that was his first career incarnation.'

Yet for all his towering self-love, many others loved him too. When Kenneth Roman wrote *The King of Madison Avenue: David Ogilvy and the making of modern advertising* (2009), few felt that the title was inaccurate or grandiose.

In 1973, Ogilvy retired as Chairman of Ogilvy & Mather and moved to Touffou, his vast estate in France. According to the company's website, he stayed in touch with the firm, and 'his correspondence so dramatically increased the volume of mail in the nearby town of Bonnes that the post office was reclassified at a higher status and the postmaster's salary raised'.

His career wasn't over, though. In 1989, the Ogilvy Group was bought by Martin Sorrell's WPP in a hostile takeover. Ogilvy famously called Sorrell uncomplimentary names. But, although there were many in advertising who were less than keen on Sorrell's way of doing things, here it was Sorrell, not Ogilvy, who knew which way the wind was blowing. Indeed, in the way that Ogilvy was a great founder of modern advertising, it was Sorrell who decades later would drag it kicking and screaming into the information age. Ogilvy was clever enough to realize that Sorrell was the new king – and Sorrell magnanimous and shrewd enough to retain Ogilvy's services. They made up, WPP became the largest communications firm in the world, and Ogilvy became Non-Executive Chairman, a position he held for three years. Only a year afterwards, Ogilvy said: 'When he tried to take over our company I would have liked to have killed him. But it was not legal. I wish I had known him 40 years ago. I like him enormously now.' Ogilvy is said to have sent Sorrell the only letter of apology he ever wrote, and the latter is supposed to have it on his office wall.

David Ogilvy died on 21 July 1999 at his home in France. He was survived by his third wife Herta Lans and a son, David Fairfield Ogilvy, from his first marriage. His name however lives on in the name of the agency he founded and in his huge influence on advertising. Moreover, thanks to the TV show *Mad Men* and its focus on this formative period, interest in Ogilvy has enjoyed something of a resurgence over the last few years.

References and further reading

Bayley, Stephen (2009) Ecstatic materialist, *New Statesman*, 23 February

Cornwell, Tim (2009) First of the madmen, *Scotsman*, 5 October

Entrepreneur (nd) David Ogilvy: master of the soft sell, profile

Gapper, John (2009) Portrait of advertising's brilliant tyrant, *Financial Times*, 26 January

Gross, Daniel (1996) *Forbes Greatest Business Stories of All Time*, pp 158–75

Hays, Constance L (1999) David Ogilvy, 88, father of soft sell in advertising dies, 22 July

Ogilvy, David (1963) *Confessions of an Advertising Man*

Ogilvy & Mather, David Ogilvy biography, www.ogilvy.com

Piggott, Stanley (1999) Obituary, *Independent*, 22 July

Roman, Kenneth (2009) *The King of Madison Avenue: David Ogilvy and the making of modern advertising*, Palgrave Macmillan, Houndmills

Time (1962) Ogilvy, the literate wizard, 12 October

Chapter Seventeen
Meg Whitman

Meg Whitman is slightly unusual in this list inasmuch as when she joined eBay it was already a pretty successful business with real prospects – and one that, unlike many dotcoms, was actually profitable. She wasn't an incomer like Ray Kroc who changed the business to the point that it may as well have been his invention. Rather she was hired as a professional CEO, and she wasn't even the first one. But, when she started in 1998, eBay had 40 employees. When she left, a decade later, it was a huge, world-girdling concern with over 10,000 employees and one of the best-known businesses on the planet.

Although she may not have been there at the genesis or have changed the company beyond all recognition, few would deny that her drive and professionalism were what made it what it is today. Under her, eBay grew faster than Microsoft, Dell or Amazon. Along with Google and Amazon, eBay is one of the three great dotcom survivors. Like both of these it has profoundly affected many people: for some the auction site is a bit of fun and a chance to pick up a bargain. For others it is how they make their living. For many businesses it is another outlet. And because the site itself is all about members selling to other members, it is not just a business, but a huge online community.

By all accounts Whitman was a pretty good boss to work for, and there are plenty of stories of her going above and beyond the call of duty and putting herself out to help staff. She also gained kudos for the comparative modesty of her pay package, although it should be noted that she owns 1.9 per cent of the company, which makes her one of the few self-made female billionaires in the world.

eBay was founded by a Frenchman of Iranian ancestry, Pierre Omidyar. He moved to the United States with his parents at the age of six and became interested in computing. After studying computer science, he worked at Claris, an Apple subsidiary, before becoming a technology entrepreneur and co-founding his own company. In 1995, aged 28, he came up with the idea for eBay and wrote the original code over the long US Labor Day weekend. He launched the site in 1995; it went by the catchy name 'Auction Web'. Omidyar had originally intended to register his site as Echobay.com, but the name had already been taken by a local mining company, so he went with eBay.com, his second choice. Auction Web was so small that it was simply part of Omidyar's larger personal site, which hosted among other things an information page on the Ebola virus.

It's a common misconception that eBay was founded to help Omidyar's fiancée swap Pez candy dispensers, but this was a PR ruse dreamt up in 1997. In fact, he built the site because he was interested in the idea of a global marketplace. Auction Web's first sale – which was really just Omidyar trying his site out – was a broken laser pointer that went for $14.83. He was so surprised that he phoned the buyer to explain that the thing didn't work. Then he discovered that, astoundingly, he had found a man who collected broken laser pointers. Initially the site was free, but it later began to charge to offset its hosting costs. The charging structure was very simple: 35 cents for listing and a small percentage of the value of the final bid price.

In 1995, Omidyar hired his first employee to help him with the day-to-day running of the site. Six months after launch, eBay was profitable, a remarkable feat in a business climate where profitability often seemed to be a shimmering mirage. The following year, he hired Jeff Skoll and quit his day job. Skoll authored the business plan that would result in the company's initial rapid growth. In

1996, the site hosted 200,000 auctions, and revenue topped $10,000 a month. In January 1997, the figure for auctions was 2 million. The same year, the Auction Web name was dropped, the company was renamed eBay, and the famous star ratings made their debut. By the end of the year, $95 million worth of sales had taken place, and the site had 341,000 users. Now it had a shot at the big time, and it needed a professional CEO with big-time experience.

Before Meg Whitman joined eBay, her life was the very model of upper-middle-class professional success. She was born in 1956 on Long Island, New York, in Oyster Bay, the youngest of three siblings, and grew up in Cold Spring Harbor. Her father ran a loans company, and her upbringing was affluent – the area is where F Scott Fitzgerald set *The Great Gatsby*, and the Whitmans had links to the Boston Brahmins, the city's WASP elite. Whitman attended the excellent local school and was an outstanding student and good at sports. In 1973 she went to Princeton University, where she intended to study medicine, but she struggled with chemistry and, instead, majored in economics. After this she went to Harvard Business School. Her classmates were an illustrious lot and would variously go on to run PepsiCo, Staples, and the New York Stock Exchange. She also met her husband, who was studying medicine; they married three years later.

After gaining her MBA, she joined Procter & Gamble in the company's consumer branding division. This did not last long, as her husband had been offered a residency in neurosurgery at the University of California. She found a job at the consultancy Bain & Co; she was hired by Mitt Romney, who would later become a rare Republican – and even rarer Mormon – governor of Massachusetts (2003 to 2007) and a presidential contender in the 2008 election. She lasted eight years at Bain and then moved to a series of companies, going from advising to doing. She became a mother and also took up a senior marketing position at Disney.

When her husband was offered the post of Chief Neurosurgeon at Massachusetts General Hospital, the couple and their two children moved to Boston; she became President of Stride Rite shoes, where she turned around the troubled Keds sneakers line. She then joined Florists' Transworld Delivery (FTD), a long-established cooperative of florists that wanted to expand and raise its profile, as President. It wasn't a happy fit, and the organization's archaic and decentralized structure frustrated her. She lasted a little over a year before leaving. She then moved back to more familiar territory – the toy maker Hasbro, where she ran its pre-school division. There she breathed new life into the venerable and ailing Playskool and Mr. Potato Head lines, which were bleeding cash. It was 1997, and the dotcom boom was well under way.

Meanwhile, on the West Coast, Pierre Omidyar and Jeff Skoll had been brainstorming potential candidates to run eBay and, as they would later say, one name kept coming up again and again. Whitman, they believed, was the ideal candidate. The question was how to tempt her out of established consumer brands into the unknown.

In the autumn of 1997 Whitman got a call from David Beirne, an executive recruiter and early backer of eBay, asking her if she was interested in being CEO. She wasn't particularly, as she'd never heard of Auction Web or eBay. She looked at the company's website – which was essentially classified ads – and it didn't particularly impress or enlighten her. However, after much convincing, she agreed to fly to California to meet Omidyar and Skoll. She changed her mind when she saw the way that a community was building around the site. 'The connection between the company and its users was something I'd rarely seen', she later told *Forbes*.

She decided she wanted the job, so, after speaking to her family, they packed up and headed back to the Bay Area. She started as eBay's CEO in February 1998. She soon forged a relationship with AOL, which helped shield the company from predatory rivals. By September of that year, she had taken the company public. Omidyar and Skoll became multibillionaires, she became a billionaire and dozens of staff became millionaires. The euphoria was short-lived, and 1999 was a rather more testing year. On 10 June, the site had an infamous meltdown, which took it offline for 26 hours. For online businesses, particularly back then, long outages raised the prospect of mass defections to other competing services. But what eBay discovered – to its great surprise – was that its community wanted to help and was largely sympathetic. Nonetheless, she resolved that technology, which had never been the company's strong suit, was going to become its core. To this end, she famously moved in with the engineers, despite knowing very little about technology, and stayed there for three months until she did.

She was also a great believer in the idea that those who ran eBay should be close to those who used it. She stipulated that executives had to auction items regularly so they understood the concerns of everyday members. She led by example, selling the contents of her ski lodge online.

Ebay

eBay has played host to some extraordinary items over the years. These include an F/A-18 Hornet jet fighter (buy-it-now price $9 million, didn't sell), one of the US Virgin Islands, a Channel Tunnel boring machine, the original Hollywood sign and a town in California. Although these may sound like jokes, many organizations, from governments to companies, have found it an effective way of getting rid of hard-to-shift items.

The site has a very frivolous side too, and is great for tabloid-style publicity. Items that have been sold include a single cornflake, a Brussels sprout and a partly eaten grilled cheese sandwich with an image of the Virgin Mary. Proving that global reach means a global market in suckers, the sandwich made $28,000. Several young women have even tried to auction their virginity on eBay.

But for some the online auction site is a very serious business indeed, and eBay is that decidedly postmodern thing – a business that itself hosts many thousands of other businesses. As at the end of 2010, the site reckons that it has hosted 127 businesses with a turnover of more than £1 million in the UK alone.

The site boomed. In 2000 it had 22.5 million users; in 2001 it had 42.4 million users; and by 2004 it had 135 million users. Whitman also took a very strategic view. First she expanded and refined the auction business; then in 2002 eBay bought PayPal for $1.5 billion, something the eBay community had pushed Whitman strongly to do. She moved the company into new markets as diverse as Germany and the Philippines, and in 2004 eBay bought a 28.4 per cent stake in the enormously successful classifieds site Craigslist. The stock reached an all-time high of $58 in 2004. But then things started to go wrong. In January the following year, the company posted lower-than-expected growth figures; it is perhaps a testament to the success of eBay that the revenue growth figures disappointed because they were under 50 per cent year on year.

It got worse though. Towards the end of 2005 eBay paid $2.6 billion for Skype, the free over-the-net telephone business. This did not go down well on Wall Street. Unlike PayPal, which was seen as a natural fit and a clear revenue generator, Skype was regarded as something that had nothing to do with eBay's core business; worse still, there was no clear path to profit for Skype. Eventually, in 2009, eBay sold a majority stake in Skype (keeping 35 per cent) for around $2 billion; it was not a great investment.

But Whitman was developing other interests too. She became politically active in 2006, through Mitt Romney, whom she had stayed friends with after she left Bain, and was involved in his campaign when he ran for the Republican nomination. When Romney withdrew from the presidential race and endorsed McCain, Whitman became co-chair of the latter's campaign; she was mooted as a potential Treasury Secretary. In 2008, she stepped down as CEO of eBay, handing the mantle over to John Donahoe, the president of eBay's Marketplaces division, whom she had recruited from Bain. Almost immediately rumours that she was going to run for the governorship of California surfaced.

Interestingly for an ex-dotcommie, Whitman ran as a Republican (much of Silicon Valley is as solidly Democrat as that other wellspring of power in California, Hollywood). She won the nomination in the summer of 2010, and came in for criticism for the amount of money she had spent doing so. In the days of the Tea Party, it's worth remembering that California Republicans, like Governor Schwarzenegger, are very much on the socially liberal side of the party. She received criticism from both the Right and the Left, and didn't win. Even if she had won, she may have wondered if it was winning at all. So dire are the Golden State's financial woes that in recent years California has struggled to pay employees and has had to issue IOUs to creditors. An odd (and ruinous) piece of legislation makes it very difficult to raise certain taxes, while powerful unions mean that cuts are likely to cause howls of anguish and alienate many. The governorship of the state is widely considered a poisoned chalice. Had Whitman won, she might have looked back at building one of the world's most successful businesses and communities as a walk in the park.

References and further reading

Brown, Erika (2007) What would Meg do? eBay's Meg Whitman does things the right way, *Forbes Asia*, 21 May

Dillon, Patrick (2004) Peerless leader: perceptive, adaptable, and remarkably low-key, eBay chief executive Meg Whitman rides e-tail's hottest segment – the global garage sale called peer-to-peer, *Christian Science Monitor*, 10 March

Holson, Laura M (1999) eBay's Meg Whitman explores management, *Web Style*, 19 May

Sunday Times (2010) Profile: Meg Whitman, 13 June

Chapter Eighteen
Mark Zuckerberg

Facebook is the greatest of the Web 2.0 companies and has become shorthand for the phenomenon called social networking. Launched in 2004, by mid-2010 it had half a billion members. Politicians, businesspeople, marketers and advertisers are in thrall to its ability to reach people, sometimes to the point where they dispense with common sense. Facebook is widely credited with having had a significant – and possibly even decisive – effect on the 2008 US election.

There were social networks before Facebook, some long before, but only one of them, Myspace, has come close to Facebook in terms of success. Facebook long ago left this earlier rival (now owned by Rupert Murdoch) in the rear-view mirror, spitting dust and indignation. Investors talk breathlessly of the company being worth $40 billion-plus and its mooted initial public offering (IPO) being bigger than Google's. It's founder, Mark Zuckerberg, is the subject of endless rumours and not a few lawsuits. He's regularly compared to Bill Gates and the Google duo.

Zuckerberg's story is, naturally enough, a fairly short one. He was born in White Plains, New York, in 1984, the second of four children. He attended his local school in Dobbs Ferry and then moved to the prestigious Phillips Academy, which traces its roots back to the

American Revolution and whose alumni read like a list of the United States' great and good. There he distinguished himself as a student with particular strength in maths, English and classics. He was captain of the school fencing team. He was also interested in computers and wrote a music player that attracted the interest of Microsoft and AOL.

Zuckerberg then went to Harvard. His interest in programming grew, expanding to include social networking software. He had a mischievous streak in him and, in 2003, created the site Facemash; apparently, the impetus for this was being dumped by a girl. Facemash was essentially an in-house version of the site Hot or Not (where users rate pictures of people based on physical attractiveness). To get his pictures, Zuckerberg hacked into Harvard's network and pulled out the ID photos. The site was popular – so popular that it crashed the university's servers, but the Harvard authorities were not amused. They shut it down, and Zuckerberg was threatened with expulsion, which he managed to avoid.

Zuckerberg continued to play around with different ideas around this theme and, in early 2004, the end result of this was called The Facebook. Within two weeks, half the students at Harvard had signed up. Initially, the site was for Harvard students only, but within a couple of months it had opened to those at Stanford, Columbia and Yale, then the entire Ivy League, and then universities across the North American continent. In 2005, the company bought the domain name Facebook for $200,000 and ditched the 'The'. Schools and some companies followed, and in 2006 the site opened to anyone over the age of 13. Traffic boomed. In 2008, it hit 100 million members; in 2009, it reached 200 million then 300 million; and in summer 2010 it crossed the half-billion mark.

In September 2009, the company said it had become cash positive. Its revenue comes largely from advertising, including an exclusive deal with Microsoft, which owns 1.3 per cent of the company (Zuckerberg owns 24 per cent); a smaller chunk of income comes from Facebook gifts (a feature that allows users to send each other virtual gifts). The company was expected to have its IPO in 2011, although a recent report from Bloomberg suggests that 2012 may be a likelier date.

However, even without an IPO, the site and its founder and CEO are never far from the headlines. Facebook has come under increasing fire from those who concern themselves with privacy and civil liberties, who often worry about the vast amounts of information Facebook captures about its users. These complaints were particularly loud in 2006, when the company introduced a news feed that kept users updated on all their friends' activities, and when it made changes to its privacy settings in 2009. Zuckerberg's response was that privacy was no longer the norm. 'People have really gotten comfortable not only sharing more information and different kinds, but more openly and with more people. That social norm is just something that has evolved over time', he told an audience in early 2010. The furore around privacy settings forced Zuckerberg to cancel a holiday in the Caribbean to celebrate his 26th birthday. Ultimately though Zuckerberg may be right: the 2006 changes are now one of the site's key features. Besides, it's hardly a secret that many Western consumers will happily trade a lot of worthy abstract ideals for a little convenience.

It's not just concerns over privacy that affect Zuckerberg's image either. There are the lawsuits. The most famous of these is the ConnectU lawsuit. This, brought by three of Zuckerberg's former classmates, essentially accuses him of stealing the idea for Facebook. It alleges that Zuckerberg was hired to write code for ConnectU and then, shortly afterwards, came up with the idea for his own networking site. After plenty of embarrassing revelations about Zuckerberg, the suit was finally settled in 2009 for a figure that could be as high as $65 million, depending on the value of the Facebook shares included in the settlement. The terms are secret. But lancing this particular boil is unlikely to make Zuckerberg's problems disappear entirely.

In 2010, Paul Ceglia, a former colleague, claimed to have a contract that showed that he owned 84 per cent of Facebook; he said that the contract was signed in 2003. Facebook has described the claim as frivolous, although it does have some echoes of the previous case and has been widely reported.

On top of this all, Zuckerberg has something of an image problem. Many see him as arrogant and disconnected, with delusions of grandeur, although there are those equally who claim this characterization is unfair. Besides, it's a little unreasonable to expect someone who is worth billions before his 30th birthday not to be affected by it in any way.

Zuckerberg ended 2010 on a slightly mixed note. On the upside, the editors of *Time* magazine considered the transformative effect of Facebook sufficient to make him their person of the year 2010, the second youngest ever after Charles Lindbergh. On a perhaps less positive note, the film *The Social Network*, an unauthorized biopic of Zuckerberg and Facebook, was a critical and commercial success.

Its tagline "You don't get to 500 million friends without making a few enemies" gives an indication of its content. Zuckerberg has said of the film "It's interesting, but it's fiction." Anyway, 500 million friends was some time ago now.

References and further reading

Arthur, Charles (2009) Facebook paid up to $65m to founder Mark Zuckerberg's ex-classmates, *Guardian*, 12 February

Ashwood, Jon and Heath, Allister (2007) Because he's worth it, *The Business*, 29 September

Burrell, Ian (2010) He's got the whole world on his site, *Independent*, 24 July

Harvey, Mike (2008) With friends like these, 110 million of them, making a profit should be easy, shouldn't it?, *Times*, 20 October

Johnson, Bobbie (2007) Profile: Mark Zuckerberg, *Guardian*, 22 July

Rivlin, Gary (2006) Wallflower at the web party, *New York Times*, 15 October

TechCrunch (2010) Interview with TechCrunch (video) on privacy, 8 January

Chapter Nineteen
Howard Schultz

If you had to pick the person who has done the most to revolutionize the retail food and drink landscape in the last 20 years, there would be few competitors for Howard Schultz. According to the company's narrative, US coffee was almost universally awful before Starbucks rode into town with its mugs of foaming latte and attractive 'third place'-style cafés. With astonishing speed coffee shops were transformed from Formica-filled places where jugs of brewed java spent hours on hotplates to attractive gathering spots for 20-somethings where all drinks were made freshly. While some might dispute some of this, there is no doubt that Schultz and Starbucks have fundamentally changed the United States' – and in many places the world's – relationship with coffee.

Of course, Starbucks did not invent the idea of coffee as a reason to gather or coffee as an espresso-based beverage, but it has done more to popularize these aspects of the drink than anyone else – and in many places it genuinely has improved the quality of what was on offer. In doing so, it has transformed high streets and shopping malls, and its distinctive green-and-white logo has become one of the world's best known. Schultz might not particularly relish the comparison, but in many ways he is the heir to Ray Kroc; the main difference is that his product is in tune with 1990s and 2000s urbanites, whereas Kroc's was aimed at 1960s and 1970s suburbanites.

Schultz was born in 1952 in a housing project in Brooklyn and grew up poor. In the United States, the projects, which are state-subsidized housing, are among the roughest places in the developed world and are a far cry from the comparatively utopian European idea of social housing. When he was seven years old, his father, who was a driver for a reusable diaper (nappy) service, broke his ankle and, as a result, lost his job. In the United States in the 1950s, where workers' rights were poor and the social safety net was near non-existent, such an occurrence might have meant not being able to feed the family. The often brutal poverty of his upbringing had a profound effect on Schultz. He has said, 'The motivation I have is, in a way, fear of failure. I didn't want to be like that. I wanted to try and build the kind of company that didn't leave people behind.'

Schultz followed a well-trodden path out of the projects. He became an athlete and excelled at sport, especially football. He was the quarterback for his high school team, and this earned him a football scholarship to Northern Michigan University. There he studied communications, graduating in 1975. After that he spent three years in sales and marketing for Xerox. In 1979, he moved to the Swedish household goods makers Hammarplast as Vice President and General Manager. Starbucks, then a coffee bean retailer, was a Hammarplast customer, and in 1981 Schultz visited the company. He was impressed by what he saw, and a year later he joined it as Marketing Director.

In 1983, Schultz visited Italy, which was an eye-opener. The country is home to an astonishing number of espresso bars – something like 200,000, for a country of under 60 million people – and he was greatly taken by the stylish Italians enjoying their espressos and cappuccinos and the way that these establishments functioned as community hubs, with people dropping in, meeting friends and chatting. Schultz thought something similar could work back in Seattle. When he returned he persuaded the owners of Starbucks to trial a café selling espresso-based drinks. They did this and it worked well, but he couldn't interest them in rolling it out.

Schultz believed in his idea enough to leave and found a rival, which he called Il Giornale. In 1987, the owners of Starbucks decided to sell the company in order to concentrate on another brand – Peet's Coffee & Tea (Peet's is still a going concern, albeit one with just under 200 retail locations, against 17,000 for Starbucks). Schultz bought Starbucks, and he was on his way. During the late 1980s the chain grew to about 50 cafés in the Seattle area, with Schultz raising capital for expansion from local investors. He soon realized there was a limit to this – to really hit the big time, he needed the financial muscle of merchant banks.

In 1991, Dan Levitan, who ran Wertheim Schroder & Co's Los Angeles office, was persuaded to pay the company a visit. Levitan came away more touched than anything else. He said that Starbucks 'was more a dream than a company' and, although he thought Schultz's devotion to his staff (stock options and healthcare for all) was cute, 'it was kind of a B plus meeting'.

But Schultz, who is credited with great powers of persuasion, managed to convince him that Starbucks was more than a cute little café. In his book *Pour Your Heart into It: How Starbucks built a company one cup at a time*, Schultz (1998) writes: '"Do you know what the problem with your business [investment banking] is?" I asked. Dan [Levitan] braced himself for a major indictment of the investment banking industry. "No, what?" he said warily. "There are not enough mensches [trustworthy people]."'

It was a bold gamble, and it paid off. Levitan invested some of his own money in the fledgling chain and, just as importantly, he bought into the idea of Schultz. A year later, his firm, along with Alex. Brown & Sons, underwrote the company's initial public offering (IPO). At the time, shares were offered for $17, and Starbucks had 193 stores. This finally gave Schultz access to the money he needed to turn his dream from a regional chain into an international one.

Over the course of the 1990s, Starbucks took over the United States and began its assault on the world. By 2000, it had around 3,500 cafés; by 2008, it had over 15,000 in 43 countries.

But soon the company started to discover that, while it's easy to be small and cute, when there's a Starbucks on every corner people feel rather differently about you. *The Simpsons* recognized this early on when, in its 1997/98 season, it featured an episode where Bart gets his ear pierced. As he walks through the mall, he passes several Starbucks. When he finally gets to In and Out Piercing, the employee says, 'Well, you better make it quick, kiddo. In five minutes this place is becoming a Starbucks.' Later, when Bart has been tattooed, he walks out of the mall to discover that every single shop is a Starbucks.

To be fair, though, Schultz pretty much stuck to his guns when it came to creating a business that treated its staff well. Despite its enormous size, Starbucks still offers medical insurance to any partner working over 20 hours a week. They still get stock options, and they get a pension plan and numerous other benefits, including a pound of coffee a week. All in all, it's a pretty impressive package, especially for what is essentially a lowly job in the service sector. It's small wonder that many Starbucks employees love the company they work for, even to the point of it feeling a bit like a cult at times. In his 2006 book *The Starbucks Experience*, Joseph Michelli offers the extraordinary tale of a regional manager who says, 'I try and set a playful and fun tone as I scrub the toilets and clean the drains.' As they say, there's employee engagement and there's employee engagement.

Schultz stepped down as CEO in 2000 and handed the reins over to Orin Smith; however, he stayed on as Chairman. While Smith took over the day-to-day running of Starbucks, Schultz decided to try his hand at turning around a professional basketball team. He bought the Seattle SuperSonics in 2001, the idea being that he would turn the team around like a business. It didn't work out like that. In 2006, he sold the team to a consortium of investors, who moved it to Oklahoma. It is no exaggeration to say that many SuperSonics fans in Seattle hated him for doing this. An ESPN sports columnist wrote of Schultz's failure to get what he wanted with the team: 'He had become angry, bitter and maddeningly defiant, like a petulant child' (Hughes, 2006).

But if his stab at sports management had gone bad at least Starbucks was riding high. Between mid- and late 2006, Starbucks shares traded at just under $40. Their IPO price had been $17; allowing for the five two-for-one stock splits, this represented capital growth of around 7,500 per cent. But it was not to last. In October 2006, the company, now with Jim Donald at the helm, saw its shares begin a decline that would last more than two years and leave them trading at under $8. Clearly something needed to be done. In January 2008, Schultz returned as CEO, telling analysts, 'Just as we created this problem, we will fix it.' But even the return of Schultz wasn't an instant fix: the shares finally stopped falling in late 2008.

It was a tough time for the chain, for while its feel-good, everyday luxury was perfectly in tune with the mores of the early and mid-2000s it was totally out of kilter with the grim economic news of the end of the decade. Many started to feel that the brand was, as the *Financial Times* (2010) put it, 'a poster child for the frothy excess of a bygone era'. There were other problems too. The company's once unassailable position as the place to go for premium coffee was under attack from both above and below. Upmarket chains were skimming off the gourmet coffee lovers who had always been rather sniffy about the firm's offerings. Meanwhile, from below, companies like McDonald's had noticed that the margins on coffee – even relatively upmarket coffee – were huge and that they could undercut Starbucks significantly on price, serve a good cup of coffee and still make stacks of cash. McDonald's went for this in a big way – never had the jibe that Starbucks was McDonald's with pretensions seemed so barbed. Schultz, to his credit, had been aware of this. In 2007 a memo from him had been leaked. In it, he warned: 'Over the past ten years, in order to achieve the growth, development, and scale necessary to go from less than 1,000 stores to 13,000 stores and beyond, we have had to make a series of decisions that, in retrospect, have led to the watering down of the Starbucks experience, and, what some might call the commoditization of our brand.'

The question was: could Schultz recapture the magic of that early 2000s Starbucks experience? He certainly wanted to. A few choice morsels from the memos he sent out after retaking the reins bore the company's trademark corporate touchy-feeliness:

- 'We are and will be a great, enduring company, known for inspiring and nurturing the human spirit.'
- 'There is no other place I would rather be than with you right here, right now!'
- 'We are in control of our destiny. Trust the coffee and trust one another.'

More pragmatically, the company was widely thought to have over-expanded, and what had once seemed like effortless dominance looked like reckless over-expansion; that famous *Simpsons* scene suddenly looked horribly prescient. Again satire had foreseen this: in 1998, the online newspaper the *Onion* ran a headline that read, 'New Starbucks opens in rest room of existing Starbucks.' The solution, in many cases, was store closures. For the most part, these were underperforming outlets, but one market was notable: in 2008, the company closed almost three-quarters of its Australian cafés. The problem, as many saw it, was that it had simply not understood the market. Nick Wailes, a strategic management expert at the University of Sydney, told *Australian Food News*, 'Australia has a fantastic and rich coffee culture and companies like Starbucks really struggle to compete with that.'

To be fair to Schultz, the coffee chain's shares have regained some of their vim, but it's difficult to escape the impression that, for Starbucks, the low-hanging coffee beans have all been picked. The company has always had its detractors. These split into three camps. The first group takes the position that Starbucks is part of the homogenization of local high streets and destroys local businesses. It's hard to refute this one; indeed, the company recently started opening unbranded stores dubbed 'stealth Starbucks', which suggests that it is aware that perhaps consumers do not want a uniform world. The second group holds that, for all its excellent benefits, the company is aggressively anti-union. Indeed, in both these senses, Starbucks is strangely contradictory. It manages to be a fairly ethical symbol of big business and a reviled symbol of globalization; it dislikes unions yet offers many of the benefits unions exist to fight for.

But it is the third criticism of Starbucks that may prove the most problematic. In 2008, Schultz wrote in his Transformation Agenda Communication #4, 'there is not a coffee company on earth providing higher quality coffee to their customers than we are. Period!' It's a fine and noble sentiment, but the trouble is there are many people who believe it to be far from the truth. Indeed, the criticism of Starbucks that stings more than any other is that the coffee really isn't that good and is very expensive to boot. Schultz may have been inspired by Italian coffee bar culture, but, so the thinking goes, if he tried to serve his coffee to the home of espresso he'd be laughed at. Others have put it more diplomatically, noting that there is little upside to the company in entering Italy. A 2008 *Which?* survey in the UK rated Starbucks as bottom of the country's high street chains, describing its coffee as poor and overpriced; it also noted that the drinks tended to be very high in calories. In short, as one blogger tartly put it, the coffee has more in common with a cup of warm ice cream than the traditional Italian espresso that inspired it. Starbucks may be a gateway to good coffee, but it is far from the final destination.

Of course, Starbucks remains a huge brand, but it now has to be a mature brand. Its first-mover advantage has gone, and it finds itself assailed on all sides by competitors that are often nimbler, cheaper or both. It has to reach new customers and deal with ever more sophisticated tastes without alienating its core. In short, its struggles are those that all the major food and beverage chains have – and to which there is no easy answer. Starbucks has a second challenge too. It desperately wants to be a good company, and its CEO deeply believes that it is, but not everyone's convinced, and when you're big it can be very, very hard to be good too.

Still, Schultz has grown a handful of Seattle coffee shops into a chain with 17,000 outlets (for comparison, McDonald's has over 31,000) in a little over 20 years. And he's done it in a way that is driven by values and employee engagement, even if many argue the extent of these. Quite where he goes from here will be interesting to see. The company's shares are currently around the $25 mark, far better than their low, but still off their peak. If Schultz can return the company to its glory days, stay ethical, deal with customer ennui and serve great coffee, then he truly is worthy of some of the more cult-like plaudits he gets from the company's baristas.

References and further reading

Allison, Melissa (2008) Starbucks shake-up: Schultz back as CEO, *Seattle Times*, 8 January

BBC (nd) Howard Schultz, profile

Clarke, Andrew (2009) The Friday interview: Starbucks boss: We're not all froth, *Guardian*, 20 March

Farrell, Greg (2010) Return of the barista-in-chief, *Financial Times*, 22 March

Hughes, Frank (2006) Why Schultz tuned out and sold the Sonics, *ESPN*, 20 July

Michelli, Joseph A (2006) *The Starbucks Experience: 5 principles for turning ordinary into extraordinary*, McGraw-Hill, New York

Pressler, Margaret Webb (1997) The brain behind the beans: Starbucks' Schultz has drawn praise, derision in building his coffeehouse empire, *Washington Post*, 5 October

Schultz, Howard (1998) *Pour Your Heart into It: How Starbucks built a company one cup at a time*, Hyperion, New York

Starbucks, www.starbucks.com

Chapter Twenty
Jack Welch

If ever a man embodied the 1990s business Zeitgeist, it was Jack Welch. Dubbed 'Neutron Jack', he was the king of shareholder value. Under him GE changed out of all recognition. Underperforming businesses were sold; new ones were acquired to bolster the balance sheet. Rather than a competitive advantage, employees were a cost like any other, and workforces could be slashed to boost margins. Managers who performed were rewarded like dukes, while those who didn't were managed out and often brutally. He deplored regulation and bureaucracy both inside and outside his company. He was the living embodiment of the celebrity CEO – the chief executive as a kind of Nietzschean *Übermensch*. Immensely pithy and quotable, he was everywhere, and everyone wanted a piece of him. He was also one of the first super-CEOs in terms of salary and was rewarded at levels his predecessors could only have dreamt of.

During his 20 years at the helm of GE, the company's value mushroomed from $13 billion to $400 billion, while profits shot up by 1,000 per cent to nearly $13 billion. In 1999, *Fortune* named him the Manager of the Century. When he left in late 2000, the plaudits piled up; Welch was a hero for our times. But his exit was brilliantly timed. The world he was CEO in was about to change with the dotcom crash, 9/11 and, later, the financial crisis of 2007–09. In hindsight, Welch's legacy looks decidedly more of a mixed-bag than it did at the time. *Fortune* may have named its Manager of the Century a little prematurely. While there is no denying that Jack Welch was one of the most influential managers of the late 20th century, whether this was a good thing or a curate's egg is now a legitimate question.

Welch was born in 1935, in Peabody, Massachusetts, the only and late son of a railway conductor and a housewife; he was a clever child and would later credit his mother with instilling a fierce ambition in him. He went on to study engineering at the University of Massachusetts and then did a doctorate in chemical engineering at the University of Illinois. In 1960, he joined GE as an engineer on $10,500 a year (about $75,000 now). After his first year, Welch was offered what he saw as an unsatisfactory pay rise of $1,000; this and his increasing impatience with the slow, bureaucratic pace of the company convinced him to quit. He even had a leaving party, but his mentor, Reuben Gutoff, drove 100 miles to have dinner with him and his wife and managed to talk him round.

Welch stayed at GE, but he didn't become a GE company man: if anything his radicalism and impatience with a conglomerate whose progress was more akin to that of a stately liner grew. Sometimes this had disastrous results – in 1963, he managed to blow up a plastics factory – but by and large his results were good enough to ensure that his foibles were overlooked. In 1969, he became General Manager of the Plastics division. On taking up his post, Welch characteristically boasted about how he would break all records, although this was not considered the done thing at GE. Indeed, his rebellious attitude and outspokenness were starting to put a few noses out of joint in the hierarchy. Nonetheless, he continued to deliver and continued to rise.

He became a Vice President of GE in 1972; in 1973, in a performance review, he wrote that his goal was to become CEO. In 1977, he assumed control of GE Credit Corporation and became a Senior Vice President. In 1979, he became Vice Chairman, and in 1981 he finally realized his ambition to become CEO of GE. Although there is no doubt that Welch had the ability and the drive to achieve this goal, some were still surprised to see him there, as he was widely considered to be too abrasive to rise to the top in what was essentially still a bureaucratic company where it didn't do to upset applecarts. However, that was exactly what Welch wanted to do, and now he was CEO there was no one to stop him.

It's worth pointing out here that, when Welch took over, he was not assuming the leadership of a struggling business that desperately needed surgery. The company was profitable and its outgoing CEO, a clubbable Englishman called Reginald Jones, greatly admired. But where many saw profitable continuity, Welch saw a sclerotic, hierarchical business that needed to be revolutionized. What happened next was the stuff of legend.

He delayered like mad, taking an axe to the company's labyrinthine bureaucracy. He sold off underperforming subsidiaries. Businesses were told that that they had to be first or second in their market – and he demanded profit growth every quarter. He embraced new management thinking, and those who impressed him were handsomely rewarded. In 1981, he gave a speech entitled 'Growing fast in a slow growth economy', which is often said to have kick-started the cult of shareholder value. Perhaps most famous was his attitude to individual performance. He was widely known for being astoundingly and even unpleasantly frank with his managers in reviews. He really wanted them to up their game, and to this end the top 20 per cent were given bonuses and share options, while every year the bottom 10 per cent were fired. This was not something Welch lost a great deal of sleep over. His stock response to the firing of the bottom 10 per cent of the workforce was that keeping them on was even crueller: 'Some think it's cruel and brutal to remove the bottom 10% of our people. It isn't. It's just the opposite. What I think is brutal and "false kindness" is keeping people around who aren't going to grow and prosper.'

In his autobiography, *Jack: Straight from the gut* (2001), he says that the company had 411,000 employees at the end of 1980 when he joined, and by the end of 1985 this figure had fallen to 299,000. Of the 112,000 who left, about a third were in sold businesses, and two-thirds were 'reduced' in continuing businesses. Indeed, so fond was Welch of slashing workforces that he earned the nickname Neutron Jack, so called because, like the then fashionable neutron bomb, he got rid of people but left the buildings standing. The workers may not have loved their new boss, but the money people did. GE's market cap soared, and Wall Street swooned. And, for all the businesses it sold, GE bought plenty too, boosting its already gigantic market value. Of course, there were downsides to all this too. In order to achieve their ever higher profit margins, managers cut areas like R&D and became risk averse. There was the human cost too, but while GE was riding high in the swashbuckling 1980s and 1990s these matters were politely ignored by those who mattered.

Soon Welch was the most talked-about – and imitated – manager in the United States. That he was extremely personable, folksy and quotable doubtless helped, but there was a lot that was concrete too. On his watch, GE became the largest and most admired company in the world. Indeed, it could sometimes seem that a cult had grown up around Welch, so ardent and uncritical were his admirers.

By the end of his tenure he was raking in a then extraordinary $4 million a year. His retirement package was generous enough to generate considerable comment, but Welch didn't care. He was a superman(ager) and he was worth it. He also scooped a $7.1 million deal for his memoirs, an extraordinary sum for a man who had not been President (in 2004, Clinton would get $10 million to $12 million).

After a lengthy and protracted succession management process, Jeffrey Immelt was chosen as Welch's successor. Welch left in late 2000, and Immelt remains in the position to this day. Much may have changed at GE, but the long tenure of its chief executives appears not to have. After GE, Welch went on to write several more books, write a very popular newspaper column, run his own company, and advise several other organizations. He has most recently been teaching a leadership course at MIT's Sloan School of Management.

With 10 years' hindsight, Welch's legacy looks perhaps a bit less golden than when he stepped down from a GE in its pomp a decade ago. At the time, there were plenty who criticized Welch for a lack of compassion and humanity and said that his easy rationale for destroying thousands of jobs was both short-sighted and cruel.

In 2001, John Cassidy wrote in the *New Yorker*: 'There were tough-guy C.E.O.s before Welch, but none of them did as much to raise Darwinism to a business philosophy. From a financial perspective – the only one that matters, he would say – Welch was a great success.' Cassidy also noted: 'Before his tenure, most G.E. employees spent their entire careers with the company, and knew they would be looked after when they retired. That company no longer exists.'

If there is a perfect summary of the downside of the business world that Reagan and Thatcher created, then this is it. But in these post-recessionary times, quite a few of Welch's other achievements seem to have lost some of their lustre. Indeed, even Welch himself has been critical of some of his more youthful nostrums. In 2009, he told the *Financial Times* that he rued his earlier obsession with shareholder value: 'On the face of it, shareholder value is the dumbest idea in the world. Shareholder value is a result, not a strategy... Your main constituencies are your employees, your customers and your products.' He added: 'The idea that shareholder value is a strategy is insane' (Guerrera, 2009).

But, in fact, the most trenchant criticism of Welch as a manager boils down to a single thing, and this is that, rather than being a genuinely great manager, he was nothing but a financial engineer on a crazed acquisition spree who was essentially taking advantage of the rather dozy way that markets valued companies, and that he knew that, as long as he delivered decent earnings growth, no one was likely to twig. His real genius, so the thinking goes, was not an aggressive, maverick approach to management. It was nothing more than a financial sleight of hand – and one he learnt by running GE Capital. Cassidy (2001) wrote, 'Truly great businessmen – such as Alfred Sloan, the creator of General Motors... do not rely on financial trickery. They build durable businesses that last for decades. Welch did no such thing.'

Certainly there is some evidence to back this up. In mid-2000, the company's shares peaked at around $60. Welch quit in November that year. The shares have never recovered and, after bobbing along for most of the 2000s at between $30 and $40, fell off a cliff in the financial crises. In 2010 they were trading at about $15. In 2009, GE was downgraded from AAA by the credit rating agencies, a rating it had held since 1956. Looked at this way, long-term, organic growth seems pretty good, and those who create slowly rather than simply buying, selling and cutting don't seem so stupid after all. Indeed, some have gone as far as to call him the man who destroyed GE, saddling it with a toxic legacy in the form of GE Capital and neutering its ability to innovate. Put like this, Welch sounds like a classic short-term manager and a slave to shareholder value rather than its master.

But then again, this very negative view is probably a little unfair on Welch. For starters we should bear in mind that he did retire in late 2000, so not all of the past 10 years can be laid at his door. We should remember too that the kind of gung-ho approach that was so loved in the 1980s, 1990s and early 2000s is probably at its most discredited right now. We should at least wait until the current revision of the period is revised. We should note too that much of what Welch did needed to be done and that during his tenure he took a deeply unfashionable business (a conglomerate) and made it into the biggest company in the world. Moreover, there were plenty of other contemporary conglomerates that not only failed to thrive, but didn't survive. So history probably won't view Neutron Jack as the man who destroyed GE – but it's unlikely to view him as the greatest manager of the 20th century either. More likely, he'll be seen as a man who symbolized an age, and one who was as much shaped by it as its shaper.

References and further reading

Byrne, John A (1998) How Jack Welch runs GE, *Businessweek*, 8 June

Cassidy, John (2001) Gut punch, *New Yorker*, 1 October

GE website, www.ge.com

Guerrera, Francesco (2009) Welch rues short-term profit 'obsession', *Financial Times*, 12 March

Hayes, Thomas C (1980) Changing the guard at GE, 28 December

McGinn, Daniel (2000) Saving Private Welch, *Newsweek*, 29 May

Nisse, Jason (2001) The lowdown: Neutron Jack flattens the bleeding hearts, *Independent on Sunday*, 14 October

Peterson, Holly (2000) How does he feel about letting people go? It is the most compassionate thing he can do, *Independent on Sunday*, 5 November

The Welch Way (official website), www.welchway.com

Welch, Jack (2001) *Jack: Straight from the gut*, Warner Books, New York

References and further reading

Chapter Twenty One
Michael Dell

Michael Dell is a spectacularly rich man – 37th on the *Forbes* list with a net worth of $13.5 billion – and because of the vagaries of share prices has been considerably richer in the past. Moreover, he became rich spectacularly early. Indeed, if you go back to the late 1990s, when Dell was in his early 30s, he was worth $10 billion; if you go back to the early 1990s, when Dell was in his 20s, you'll find plenty of articles about how he made so much so young. Although the internet boom boosted his wealth enormously, it did not create it. Indeed, he founded his company in 1984, and it took off long before most people knew what a dotcom was.

Dell's big idea was hardly rocket science. He would sell computers direct to customers, cutting out intermediaries. It doesn't sound radical, but it was at the time. Dell himself is said to be a very measured man. His entrepreneurial drive (and an enormous fortune) aside, he is a very normal and private person. He's not even ordinary in the sense that people like Warren Buffett are – look up Dell's quotes and there's not much in the way of memorable folksy wisdom. He is straightforward and down to earth, and his company reflects this. He sells what has become a commodity item. Dells are the workhorses of the computing world – solid, good value and dependable. Of course, they will sell you high-end machines if you want, but Dell is where you go if you want an ordinary computer at a keen price.

Dell was born in 1965 to solidly middle-class parents. His father was a doctor and his mother a stockbroker. They had lived in New York, but in the early 60s moved to Houston looking for a calmer life. As a child Dell demonstrated early entrepreneurial flair. Aged 12, he made $2,000 by creating his own stamp auction and advertising in a stamp collectors' journal. This, he has said, taught him the value of cutting out intermediaries. At 16, he landed a summer job selling subscriptions to the *Houston Post*. By collecting feedback on who bought subscriptions, he realized he had a vastly higher hit rate with newlyweds and those who'd just moved in. He paid friends to look for these people and targeted them with letters. That year, he earned $18,000, which he spent on a new BMW.

The Dell story really begins when he went to college – and this is the stuff of entrepreneurial legend, for one of the world's biggest computer companies really was started in a college dorm room. In 1983, aged 18, Dell was a freshman at the University of Texas at Austin taking pre-med courses. He'd had an interest in computers since he was young. The IBM-type computers that were becoming the de facto standard were quite modular in design. Dell realized that he could buy spare components from local retailers, add them to computers and then sell the souped-up, custom machines for a healthy profit; indeed, soon he was making a small fortune. In 1984, he created a business called PCs Limited, headquartered in his student room.

The reason this business worked so well was that retailers at the time had to order quotas of PCs and components from IBM and frequently had excess stock, which they were happy to sell to Dell. He then sold direct through ads in papers and magazines, allowing him to undercut retailers. This didn't go down well with his parents, who were concerned about the effect on his studies. Dell made them a promise: if the business started to struggle he'd go back to his books. Instead he was soon making about $80,000 a month. He never returned for his sophomore year, and instead tapped his family for $300,000 to expand. In 1985, the company launched its first machine, the Turbo PC. PCs Limited was already recognizable as the company it would become – it advertised in the press and sold direct to customers. Each PC could be customer specified by the buyer. This has long been one of Dell's trademarks – the concept of mass customization. As each computer is built to order from a menu of options, waste and inventories are largely eliminated – and customers are happy, as they get more or less exactly what they need. The direct approach had other obvious benefits too – it meant he could offer lower prices and make higher profits. Soon the company changed its name to Dell Computer Corporation.

The company grew quickly. In 1987, it opened a UK subsidiary, and in 1988 it went public. Shares were priced at $8.50, and Dell was 23 years old; the company he created was worth around $80 million. In 1989 it had reported sales of $257.8 million. When Dell was 24, *Inc.* magazine named him its Entrepreneur of the Year. In 1990, Dell opened a manufacturing plant in Ireland – one of the earlier examples of inward investment that would characterize the 'Celtic Tiger' economy. In 1989, the company's first laptop appeared, and in 1992 the company joined the Fortune 500. Dell was the youngest Fortune 500 CEO ever, still comfortably in his 20s. The company did have a couple of mishaps during this period – in 1990 it made some bad chip choices, and its early laptops were problematic – but these were comparatively minor setbacks.

It's worth noting here that, although Dell was in the right place at the right time and hit on an idea that in retrospect seems obvious, he was an incredibly hard worker. In his 20s, he reportedly worked 18-hour days, often seven days a week. He only cut back on this punishing schedule once he had children and at the insistence of his wife.

In the mid-1990s Dell went from big to huge. Growth in the PC market in the early 1990s had been non-existent, as the effects of the recession were still working their way through, and 1993 was a particularly bad year for the company. Soon afterwards things started to pick up again as the internet took off. Whereas previously a home PC had been something to write letters on, organize your finances with, and play a few games on, it was becoming much, much more. The PC market exploded, and with it Dell's fortunes. By 1995, the shares had gone up to $100. In 1996, the company launched dell. com; soon the site was doing $1 million worth of business a day. In 1997, it shipped its 10 millionth computer. By 2000, it was doing $50 million a day through the website, and the following year it became the biggest computer maker by market share.

The company was also diversifying. After its early teething troubles, its laptops became a huge success – and laptops are very profitable. It has also moved into the markets for servers and peripherals such as printers and monitors. The company was rather unusual in several unexpected ways. Instead of locating its factories in low-cost Asia, it based them largely in the West, which allowed it to respond very quickly with its built-to-order machines. Dell was also a very early adopter of green policies in an industry that has often been accused of neglecting the environment.

As with many other technology firms, Dell's all-time share price highs were around the peak of the dotcom boom. It suffered a sharp fall in the bust – but not that sharp, as it was hardware not vapourware – and towards the middle of the decade it rallied considerably. In 2004, Dell stepped down as CEO, although he stayed on as Chairman. Dell and his wife have become pretty big philanthropists too, if not quite in the Buffett and Gates league. They both contributed the maximum allowable contribution to George W Bush's re-election campaign – although, as they know the Bushes and are Texans, this is perhaps less notable than it may appear.

Towards the end of the 1990s, the company's fortunes suffered a sharp reverse, and what had once been its competitive advantages now became its Achilles' heels. When Dell stepped down, the company was selling more computers in the United States than its four biggest rivals combined. But soon the tables turned and HP, once a sickly second, was top dog. The reason for this was the rise of the consumer laptop, its smaller sibling the netbook and other digital devices that allowed people to access the web. The trouble was that consumers liked to buy these items in stores, where they could see them before they bought. Moreover, as laptops do not benefit from 'mass bespoking', suddenly the US factories were a high cost rather than a source of competitive advantage. Dell has also been historically weak on the consumer gadget side – and, as Apple had shown, there was huge money to be made there.

In 2007, at the request of the board, Dell returned as CEO and to a much tougher environment than the one he'd left, with not only his company on the back foot but a financial crisis. However, he did make big changes. He struck deals with retailers such as Walmart, and he revamped the company's notebook and sub-notebook ranges. (Other innovations such as the company's championing of Linux were less successful.) He opened plants in China. The results have been far from a quick fix, but slowly the company does seem to be turning around: it recently pushed Acer back to number three and regained the number two spot. Whether or not it can regain the pole position remains to be seen. Indeed, it's interesting to note that Dell, like so many company founders (eg Jobs and Schultz), has found himself having a second go at the top job after the business he created foundered once he had left.

References and further reading

Arthur, Charles (2000) The all American Dell boy, *Independent*, 29 March

Corcoran, Elizabeth (1998) Dell gives what people want, *Washington Post*, 8 July

Corcoran, Elizabeth (1998) The direct approach: thriving Michael Dell keeps honing PC sales tactics, *Washington Post*, 1 July

Dell, Michael S (2000) *Direct from Dell*

Hoover's, Profile: Dell Inc

http://www.portfolio.com/executives/features/2008/06/16/Michael-Dell-Returns-to-Dell-Inc/

Insana, Ron (2004) Dell knows his niche and he'll stick with it, *USA Today*, 5 April

Lynn, Matthew (1998) PC whizz kid piles up the billions, *Sunday Times*, 26 April

Processor.com, Dell timeline

Reischel, Diane (1990) Michael Dell: he wasn't a people person but he knew PCs. Now he's programmed that talent to become a computer mogul at 24, *Dallas Morning News*, 28 January

Shack, Justin (2010) Dell's revival runs into trouble, *Wall Street Journal*, 28 November

Sunday Times/Calgary Herald (2003) Computer tycoon lives in fear, 5 January

Vanity Fair, Michael Dell

Chapter Twenty Two
Tom Peters!

Is Tom Peters bonkers? A lot of people seem to think so – maybe even Tom Peters himself. More serious questions are: Is he any good? Is a he proper management thinker? Why is he so successful? Why is he so popular? These are all good questions and all questions we need to ask about the extraordinary phenomenon that is Tom Peters.

In an era when everyone from waste disposal companies, to consultancies, to local government subcommittees goes on about the quest for and journey towards 'excellence', it's easy to forget that what is now possibly the greatest of all management clichés was largely the responsibility of one man. In a world where most bookshops have entire sections given over to that peculiarly modern hybrid the management self-help book, it's worth remembering that just over a generation ago this industry barely existed. In a culture where everyone recognizes (even if they despise) the value and usefulness of celebrity, it's strange to reflect that a management consultant (from McKinsey & Co of all places) did back in the early 1980s. Certainly no management guru had ever used the exclamation mark as he did before.

In late 1982, *In Search of Excellence* by Tom Peters and Robert Waterman was published and changed the way management gurus were viewed for ever. What was previously a staid cottage industry was suddenly thrust into the limelight. *In Search of Excellence* was, by any standards, an incredible bestseller, shifting around 3 million copies in its first four years. It turned one of its authors into a household name and made Tom Peters a megastar. Yet for all Peters's popularity, which has endured pretty solidly in the three decades since, there are plenty who denounce him as a flashy, fame-hungry charlatan, an empty suit who is nothing but style over substance; indeed, sometimes Peters himself even says these things. In a funny way, both his supporters and his detractors are probably right.

Peters was born in Baltimore, Maryland, in 1942 (with a lacrosse stick in his hands, according to his website). His father worked for the Baltimore Gas Company and his mother was a teacher. He attended Maryland's well-known Severn School and studied at Cornell University, where he gained a Bachelor's and then a Master's degree in civil engineering, having originally wanted to be an architect. In 1966, he was deployed to Vietnam as a Navy Seabee (the Navy's engineering corps, which built structures like bridges); his second tour of duty (which his bio notes he 'survived') was in the Pentagon, and he was discharged in 1970. His time in the military had a profound influence on what he would subsequently write about management, and he later said that his two tours of duty were the best management training he could possibly have had.

After Vietnam, the Navy paid for him to go to Stanford, where he did an MBA and then a PhD in decision science and organizational behaviour. After Stanford, he took another interesting turn: from 1973 to 1974, he was a White House Drug Abuse Advisor. After all this, he finally found his calling. He joined McKinsey & Co in 1974; he would later say that he fell into management consultancy entirely by chance.

It was his work there in the 1970s that formed the basis of *In Search of Excellence*. Specifically, it was an assignment he and Waterman were given in 1977 called the Organisation Project. The duo were then based in the San Francisco office, which was seen as a backwater, and the project wasn't seen as terribly important. (In fact, it had a much more highly regarded sibling, which went nowhere.) Nonetheless, Peters was allowed (and funded) to travel the world and talk to people about teams and organizations. In 1979, the year he became a partner, he was asked to create a presentation based on his findings for Siemens; he came up with 700 slides (Peters is legendary for his slide presentations). On the back of this, he was asked to come up with something more succinct for PepsiCo. This is how he came up with his eight themes (see box).

In search of excellence: Peters and Waterman's eight common themes for successful companies

1. A bias for action and active decision making – 'getting on with it'.

2. Closeness to the customer – learning from the people served by the business.

3. Autonomy and entrepreneurship – fostering innovation and nurturing 'champions'.

4. Productivity through people – treating rank-and-file employees as a source of quality.

5. A hands-on, value-driven management philosophy that guides everyday practice – management showing its commitment.

6. Stick to the knitting – stay with the business that you know.

7. Simple form, lean staff – some of the best companies have minimal headquarters staff.

8. Simultaneously loose–tight properties – autonomy in shop-floor activities plus centralized values.

Peters would later say that he and his co-author missed the need for speed and the growing importance of globalization.

In 1981, Peters left McKinsey to found his own consultancy, and the following year he published *In Search of Excellence* (*ISOE*) with a fellow McKinseyite, Robert Waterman. The book took 43 US companies that Peters and Waterman had studied while at McKinsey and told exciting stories about how they had achieved excellence. In a time when management books were as dry as desert tombs, *ISOE* was highly accessible.

The critical reaction to *ISOE* was hardly unanimous acclaim. Plenty of reviewers took umbrage at the book's style. The *New York Times* review said:

> No, these are not a series of exhortations badly translated from the instructions to a Japanese toy. These are the authors' solutions to America's present productivity crisis. This is why I say: if the language that Mr. Peters and Mr. Waterman speak is any accurate reflection of the American businessman's current thinking, then we are deep in the cauldron with the water very near the boiling point.

The reviewer did have the decency to add, 'Lost in the syntactical fog of *In Search of Excellence* is a good idea for a book.'

Perhaps the harshest criticism of all though came from the pair's fellow consultants. Many at McKinsey viewed it as cheap populism that demeaned the serious work they did. Peters would later say that nothing prepared him for the vicious attacks of his former colleagues. But ultimately it didn't really matter what the people at the firm or the *New York Times* thought: the business elite's sneers may have hurt him, but they didn't hurt sales. His book was a blockbuster, not a scholarly tome, and was a greater success than its authors (or publishers, or anyone else) could have imagined.

Peters's timing was exquisite. In 1982, the United States was suffering from a period of introspection and insecurity (which incidentally was quite closely mirrored by its 2010 post-banking crisis funk). The country had endured defeat in Vietnam and then watched its industrial greatness stagnate in the 1970s. There had been the disappointing Carter presidency, and then there was the Reagan recession of the early 1980s. In those long-ago days, it seemed that Japan might take over the world. (Famously at the height of Japan's economic muscle the grounds of the Imperial Palace in Tokyo were reckoned to be worth more than all of California.) Americans wanted people who could tell them that they could be great again and on their own terms. (They had, after all, just chosen Reagan over Carter.)

However, it wasn't just this. The US market for self-help books was about to take off too. Peters and Waterman found themselves riding on the crest of a double wave. To be fair, Peters himself was aware of this and would later say that *ISOE* was a 'a decent book with perfect timing'. Indeed, the book became the first management title ever to grab the number one spot on the *New York Times* bestseller list. Its sequel, *A Passion for Excellence*, was the second. The two authors were clearly very different men: the ebullient (and some might say egotistical) Peters used the book as a launch pad to superstardom. The more staid Waterman remained a management consultant at McKinsey, and then headed off to run his own company. Collectors of managerial trivia may be interested to know he also chairs the Restless Leg Foundation.

Peters quickly discovered he had a taste for the limelight and took the opportunity to turn himself into something entirely new – the management guru as a celebrity. In a 2000 piece, *Red Herring* magazine wrote:

> During the middle of that decadent decade, while Michael Jackson was moonwalking up the MTV charts, Mr. Peters was rocketing to rock-star status in the multimillion-dollar business-guru industry he created almost single-handedly... But Mr. Peters proved more than just an author; almost overnight, he blossomed into a live performer on the scale of Elvis. By his own estimate, in 1985 he gave more than 150 of his raucous seminar-cum-revival meetings, sometimes storming through two cities a day. By the end of the decade, he was commanding as much as $50,000 per appearance, assuring his status as the undisputed, all-time uberguru.

Peters was a machine. *A Passion for Excellence* was followed by *Thriving on Chaos, Liberation Management, The Pursuit of WOW* and the *Tom Peters Seminar: Crazy times call for crazy organizations*.

All were direct and obvious and had a kind of cheesy populism about them – and all sold by the truckload. In total, since 1982, he's written 14 books, which would be a pretty decent life's work for most people, but this was on top of an unbelievably hectic schedule of speaking events and appearances for which he was paid sums most consultants could only dream of.

As the 1980s turned into the 1990s, plenty of people began to voice the view that, even if he may have sort of had a point once, Peters had gone (to use a word he was fond of) bonkers. How could you take a man with this kind of kindergartenish energy, whose pronouncements seemed so crazy, seriously – especially when he seemed to get it wrong so often? But instead of rejecting these barbs, Peters often agreed with them. One of his own descriptions from the era was, 'a prince of disorder, champion of bold failures, maestro of zest, professional loudmouth, corporate cheerleader, lover of markets, capitalist pig, and card-carrying member of the ACLU'.

Some criticism was rather more measured and substantial though. In 1984 *Businessweek* ran a cover story entitled 'Oops! Who's excellent now?', which noted that a third of Peters's 43 excellent companies were struggling within five years of having been designated excellent by Peters. Later, in 2001, *Fast Company* ran a piece suggesting that some of the data in the surveys may have been faked. In a peculiar twist, the piece was bylined to Peters himself, although it subsequently turned out to be an 'as told to'. In 2003, the *Evening Standard's* Chris Blackhurst (2003) wrote, '[Peters is] probably the propagator of more twaddle than anyone on the planet.' Blackhurst also noted that Peters's deeper problem was that his own record was 'so suspect' and that he used his mistakes to make even more money, adding that 'He wants his tombstone to read, "Thomas Peters – he was a player." He was that, all right. Whether he was any good is a different matter.'

As cited in the *Economist* (2009) Kathryn Harrigan, Professor of Business Leadership at Columbia Business School, memorably said of *ISOE*: 'Americans are into cults, particularly the cult of the personality. They are all looking for the recipe of success, and Tom Peters made the best job of that. People knew exactly where to place him.' Meanwhile, the *Economist* (2009) weighed in with: 'He peddled his theories of excellence with the exuberance and evangelistic zeal of a 19th-century cough-syrup salesman.'

But again, rather than rebut criticism, Peters revelled in it. In a 2008 interview with the *Financial Times*' Stefan Stern, he said:

> I say to people, 'You got a bad deal, paying money to see me. I have utterly nothing new to say. I am simply going to remind you of what you've known since the age of 22 and in the heat of battle you forgot.' You'd have to be one of those television preachers to believe that you're going to work with a group of 500 people and change their lives. First of all, most of them agree with you. You're not going to pay £1,000 [a head] to go and see someone if you think the guy's a jerk.

Indeed, he can sometimes seem completely incorrigible. When asked about a story in *Fortune* that claimed he'd lost his mind, he replied: 'At the peak of the internet bubble you had a market cap for Microsoft three times the size of IBM. So that's kind of bonkers! That's kind of my message! You should be bonkers in a bonkers time!' He's also said, 'I'm proud of the inconsistency too! Being totally consistent in the face of dramatic challenges is silly!' Yet although this does sound ridiculous and as though Peters is trying to have it both ways, there may be a kernel of a deeper truth here – that 'management thinking' is often nothing like the hard, predictive science many of its more po-faced practitioners believe it to be. After all, if getting things wrong was sufficient to destroy reputations, business school management departments would resemble the *Mary Celeste*.

Then again, perhaps we're looking at this the wrong way. Tom Peters may not act like a serious management thinker. That could be because he isn't one. Rather he's a mix of management guru, self-help expert, motivational speaker and born-again preacher. Whatever the case, Peters and his legions of fans remain entirely untroubled by these matters, and Peters continues to rake in the cash.

This may be the most infuriating thing of all for his detractors. There must be nothing more galling than to watch someone knock about like a pop star, put out stuff that you consider is pretty lightweight, even admit to people that it's kind of rubbish – and then outsell more serious authors by a factor of 100. 'Serious' management looks at Peters with a peculiar mix of contempt, astonishment and envy. Still, this has been the story of high art versus low art for hundreds of years, and there's no reason that what's true of books and theatre shouldn't be true of management.

Perhaps then those who practise *haute* management should take the same view. Peters has many of the attributes of a cheesy populist entertainer. It's a bit like Clive James's famous quip about Barry Manilow: 'Nobody you know likes him, but everyone you don't know thinks he's great.' Tom Peters – the Barry Manilow of management.

References and further reading

Blackhurst, Chris (2003) Master of reinvention, *Evening Standard*, 1 October
Economist (2009) Guru: Tom Peters, 26 March
Gibb, Robina (1998) Listen to my story, *Scotsman*, 23 May
Leonard, Carol (1992) Millionaire marketing guru who reigns supreme, *Times*, 5 December
Parker, Ciaran (2006) *The Thinkers 50: The world's most important and influential business thinkers*, London Business Press, London
Peters, Tom and Waterman, Robert (1982) *In Search of Excellence: Lessons from America's best-run companies*, Harper & Row, New York
Red Herring (2000) The 1980s will be remembered for many things: leveraged buyouts..., 1 September
Seid, Dennis (2007) In search of Tom Peters, *Northeast Mississippi Daily Journal*, 2 November
Stern, Stefan (2008) It's about getting stuff done: lunch with the FT, *Financial Times*, 22 November
Tom Peters website, www.tompeters.com

Chapter Twenty Three
Ricardo Semler

Ricardo Semler is probably best known for his 1993 book *Maverick! The success story behind the world's most unusual workplace*. Titles in business publishing are much given to hyperbole, but Semler is the genuine article. He is unorthodox and iconoclastic, arguably the strangest and most original CEO of the 1990s. He tore up the rule book, and told his staff they could do whatever they wanted. Compared to him, most so-called business radicals are conservatives who tinker around the edges.

Over the years his company, Semco, has been a kind of strange industrial laboratory where the response to the oddest management notions always seems to have been 'Yes, let's try it.' He took empowerment as far as it could possibly go – to the point where he basically let the workers run the business. Nobody expected it to work. But it did – and brilliantly. As the British management thinker Charles Handy wrote, 'The way that Ricardo Semler runs his company is impossible; except that it works, and works splendidly for everyone.' Yet for the thousands of consultants who have crawled over his company and the hundreds of articles that have been written about his way of doing things, Semco remains unique. For all the success of Semler's radicalism, it has not been imitated. Indeed, this bizarre and rather wonderful Brazilian company exists as a kind of organizational utopia, a reminder of how things could be, rather than how they are.

Semler's early years were those of a typical child of the Brazilian elite. His father, an Austrian by birth, founded Semco in the 1950s, and the business became an industrial concern making industrial pumps and compressors; it was reasonably successful, but in no way remarkable. The young Ricardo was clearly bright and – unlike many of the princelings he grew up with – had a strong drive to get things done. He was turned down by Harvard twice because he was too young and eventually gained a place by writing to the rector and pointing out that, in the past, 14-year-old monarchs had run whole countries. Semler says that he was the youngest person ever to go to Harvard Business School.

In 1982, at the age of 21, he took over his father's factory. It's true that 21 is a pretty callow age to do such a thing, but Semler's father could see his son was restless and he didn't want him to seek his fortune elsewhere. He is also reported to have said, 'Better make your mistakes while I'm still alive.' At the time, Semco was a pretty standard hierarchical business, which employed a fair number of Semler's relatives; it was, in short, the Latin American norm, and Semler started out being a pretty normal CEO.

But clearly the 21-year-old had a lot to prove – especially as, in the early 1980s, the Brazilian economy was in a terrible state. So Semler started out by trying to learn everything he could about the company, travelling around the world and working 16-hour days. The workload soon took its toll: while visiting a factory in New York State, he collapsed. Doctors found nothing wrong with him, but advised him that his lifestyle was a ticket to an early heart attack.

Semler took note and resolved to improve his work–life balance. He had been an obsessive micromanager and detail person. Now, he started wondering what would happen if he was the exact opposite. What if, rather than keep tabs on everyone, he told them they could do whatever they wanted? If he made everyone completely responsible for their actions, would they act responsibly? Could real industrial democracy work? This, in a nutshell, was Semler's vision. In 1983, he began plotting to democratize his father's business. Many right across the company, from top to bottom, were not impressed with his plans, and he eventually bought a number of family board members out.

In some ways, what he proposed doesn't sound that radical today. It was about profit sharing, empowerment of workers and making the workplace human, but where Semler differed is that he took every single one of these ideas to its logical extreme. That was piercingly, sweepingly radical. It's also worth remembering that he did it in early 1980s Brazil, where the typical management hierarchy was something the Victorians would probably have felt pretty comfortable with.

He split the business into highly autonomous factory units. He delayered the hierarchy, leaving only three levels between the top and the shop floor, and he abolished all titles – anathema in status-conscious South America. Semler basically inverted the management pyramid. Anyone could look at the company's books. Workers assessed management's performance, including his own. It was industrial democracy. In 1988, in the *Financial Times*, Laura Leme, who worked at head office, said, 'There was resistance from both above and below. Brazilian society is extremely authoritarian. People at the bottom didn't want the responsibility and many managers just couldn't get used to having their orders challenged. From October 1985 to January 1987, a third of the management left. Then things improved.'

Semler became one of six counsellors who took it in turn to be CEO. All managers were rated by their staff – drop to low and you went, and this applied to Semler too (although he did own the lion's share of the company). Staff set their own salaries. Industrial units were allowed to employ no more than 100 people; anything larger was broken up, meaning you could have several units operating on one site. They were allowed to come and go as they pleased; as they voted to abolish clocking in and clocking out they could work from home; they could become consultants. Staff could vote on whether or not to employ people. Profit sharing was instituted and in a big way – at 15 per cent. By the late 1980s, it was working – and working well.

Semler's six principles

1. Don't increase the business size unnecessarily.
2. Never stop being a start-up.
3. Don't be a nanny to your workers.
4. Let talent find its place.
5. Make decisions quickly and openly.
6. Partner promiscuously; you can't do it all yourself.

In 1988, Semler published his first book, *Virando a Propria Mesa* (Turning the Tables). It sold 45,000 copies in three months. The book was not complimentary about the Brazilian industrial establishment and conventional wisdom: it said Brazilian business was conservative, designed to serve vested interests, and would wither and die when the country opened its gates to foreign competition. Next came an interview with *Veja*, the country's best-known weekly news magazine, where he lambasted the business establishment anew. As the *Financial Times* said, 'All this could be treated as the rantings of a spoilt child if it were not for Semler's remarkable success as a businessman.' Indeed, all those praying for this industrial upstart to fall flat on his face would be sorely disappointed: in 1980, Semco had sales of $4 million. By 1987, it had sales of $39 million. Growth, by any standards, was impressive and by Brazilian standards was nothing short of astonishing.

Moreover, the company had diversified from its simple base into dozens of areas.

The Semco story got stranger still – by 1993, the company had only 200 people on the payroll. The rest were indirectly employed either as consultants, operating their own businesses within the business, or self-employed and often working remotely. Semler went from *enfant terrible* to a man the establishment admired and wanted to learn from. He was voted Brazilian Businessman of the Year in 1990 and again in 1992. The company was hailed as the most successfully re-engineered business in the world; its success was all the more remarkable when you consider the state of the Brazilian economy, which had experienced hyperinflation in the early 1990s.

What really brought Semler to the notice of the wider world though was the 1993 publication of *Maverick!*, which was a version of *Virando a Propria Mesa*. It became a global business bestseller. As with many publishing phenomena, its timing was right. The West had long been importing foreign business wisdom from Japan, but the Asian superstar had lost its lustre and just entered its lost decade. Moreover, the first stirrings of the dotcom revolution were being felt. There was a keen appetite for new ideas, and a Brazilian radical fitted the bill perfectly. *Maverick!* made Semler into a media superstar, and business audiences lapped him up. Semler would follow this book with *The Seven Day Weekend: Changing the way work works* in 2003.

During the 2000s, Semler's involvement in the strange and rather wonderful company he'd created (or re-engineered) decreased. In many ways this was inevitable – by ceding so much power to others, he'd made being CEO into a part-time job. The company was basically running itself, and he joked that he was more or less unemployed. By 2003, Semco had annual revenues of $212 million or roughly 50 times what they'd been when the 21-year-old Semler took up the reins. In terms of other more Semleresque measures of success, employee turnover was under 1 per cent a year.

Luckily, he had other interests, and he turned his attentions to education. He'd spent seven years looking at democratic schools and, in 2003, opened an institution in Sao Paolo called the Lumiar School, which used many of the ideas that made Semco such a success and repurposed them for the education of Brazil's youth. There were no classrooms, no homework, no learning what you didn't want, and no teachers, but instead full-time mentors and part-time experts. Nor was Semler's radical experiment in education some kind of privileged hothouse for the children of the wealthy; rather, 75 per cent of the pupils were scholarship children from poor backgrounds. There are now three of these schools. His other activities include the promotion of industrial democracy and environmental causes.

Semler and Semco are both undoubtedly great successes, but there is one great question hanging over all this. If these ideas are so brilliant, why aren't they everywhere? Why is Semco still a brilliant one-off? Semler himself has attempted to answer this question. In a 1993 interview with the *Guardian*, he said, 'The main problem afflicting all these companies is autocracy. America, Britain and Brazil are very proud of their democratic values in civic life, but I have yet to see a democratic workplace. That is the difficult transition that is going on. We are still constricted by a system that doesn't allow democracy into the business or the workplace' (Keegan, 1993). He has also said, 'There is nothing in the system to help people make the leap of faith to let go of control. I know that as I let things deconstruct it will turn out better, but many do not know this. Giving up control is something none of us do well in any aspect of our lives.'

He has also suggested that another reason Semco is not widely imitated is that other companies that try it wind up taking the road of collectivism. He also notes that, during the dotcom boom, it seemed as if his anarchic but democratic model might finally have its moment in the sun. 'They said: this Semco thing fits! They had beanbags in reception. But it didn't go anywhere. As soon as their businesses started getting serious, they started having corner offices and two secretaries.' There is certainly something to this, and it chimes with another of his observations that might be closer to the truth: that the system we have throws up the wrong kind of leaders, the kind of gung-ho, ambitious and driven but slightly sociopathic and emotionally backward male executive who is everyone's comedy MBA stereotype.

There is truth here too. One of the greatest reasons that there are no more Semlers is likely to be because people like Semler do not rise far in most companies. Paradoxically, then, the only person in a position to institute industrial democracy is someone who inherited his job. Semler was a kind of industrial Gore Vidal – and those best placed to mock and subvert an elite often come from within it. They understand the way it works and are unimpressed by the trappings of power. However, you also need character and intellect – and few scions of wealthy families try to tackle the system to which they owe their position. Semler had both character and intellect, and they made him a true oddity – half-businessman, half-philosopher or thinker. Few people are given the chance to run a serious company at 21 – and of those a tiny subset are likely to want to overturn every applecart and machinegun entire herds of sacred cows. If you think about it, it's almost impossible to think of someone else in business quite like him; maybe there really is only one Ricardo Semler.

Of course, it's worth remembering that many of the ideas he has championed have found a wider audience and that thousands of companies have taken a pick-and-mix approach to some of what he's done, but no others have bought into it wholesale – or at least not successfully. For the most part Semco exists as a brilliant example of what could be rather than what is.

References and further reading

Caulkin, Simon (1993) The boy from Brazil – Ricardo Semler, *Observer*, 17 October

Dawnay, Ivo (1998) Management: at odds with a Latin culture – why Ricardo Semler is a novelty in Brazilian industry, *Financial Times*, 11 November

Dawnay, Ivo (1998) Survey of the state of Sao Paolo (11): corporate enfant terrible, *Financial Times*, 15 September

Downie, Andrew (2004) Learn what you want, *Daily Telegraph*, 9 February

eWeek (Ziff Davis Media) (2004) Ricardo Semler: set them free, 30 April

Financial Times (1988) At Odds With a Latin Culture, 11 November

Gardner, Darren (2003) A boss who's crazy about his workers, *Sunday Herald*, 13 April

Keegan, Victor (1993) Has work reached the end of the line? Semco, *Guardian*, 28 September

Kellaway, Lucy (2003) How and why of the workers' paradise, *Financial Times*, 14 April

Management (2007) In touch: Ricardo Semler: still a maverick, 1 April

Chapter Twenty Four
Herb Kelleher

Many industries have been transformed in the last 20 years. The airline industry is one of them, but its transformation has been rather unusual. Many sectors that have changed beyond all recognition – such as music or newspapers or video – have done so because technology has completely rewritten the rules for them. Others – such as food – have been radically altered because of changing public tastes. But the airline industry does exactly the same thing as it did 30 years ago. It still flies people from A to B for the same reasons they've always flown – and although planes are more advanced they're still recognizably planes, and plenty of 20-year-old aircraft are still in service.

The airlines' big change has been going from being a comparatively expensive high-end industry to a cheap, low-margin, mass-market one. Until the end of the 1980s, flying was still pretty expensive. Ordinary people did not, as a rule, fly to Spain for the weekend or to New York to do some shopping. Yet all this was about to start changing, and the world we now have where flights can cost as little as a cup of coffee – and where the elegance of the golden age of aviation really is a dim and distant memory – is largely down to one man and one company. These are Herb Kelleher and Southwest Airlines. The company served as the model for all the Ryanairs and easyJets and SpiceJets and Dragonairs. It was the first of the budget airlines – and a lot of people think it is still the best.

It may also come as a surprise to non-Americans, but it was until recently the largest airline in the world by passenger volume – and, although none of its planes travel beyond the United States and Canada, it puts on over 3,200 flights a day. It also routinely tops customer satisfaction polls. In a world where airlines are struggling and going out of business, Southwest's balance sheet is in rude good health and always has been. Interestingly, the biggest international carrier (using the passenger metric) is Ryanair, whose business model is more or less a carbon copy of Southwest's (see box). The airline even has a phenomenon named after it, 'the Southwest effect', where the entry of the airline or similar to a community lowers fares, boosts service and results in increased air travel.

Ryanair

Southwest has spawned numerous imitators around the world. In fact, the pace of imitation has largely been driven by deregulation – the moment a market deregulates, a host of Southwest mini-mes crop up. Probably the most notable of these, though, is the Ireland-based Ryanair, which was directly inspired by Southwest (Michael O'Leary visited Southwest and then applied the model to his airline). But, cheapness aside, the two organizations are quite different, and much of this stems from the characters of their respective CEOs. While Kelleher is all folksy charm, O'Leary is perhaps best known for his 'attitude', which is along the lines of 'You get what you pay for and nothing more.' O'Leary is one of the world's most acerbic CEOs and takes great delight in telling his customers exactly what he thinks. Some of his more memorable quotes include 'The European consumer would crawl naked over broken glass to get low fares' and 'We don't fall all over ourselves if they say my granny fell ill.' He has famously suggested that he would like to charge passengers for using the toilet and that co-pilots are an expense that he would like to cut, but he has not put people off: Ryanair is now the largest low-cost airline in Europe. Its cavalier attitude, he says, is the price you pay for the democratization of flying: 'Now everyone can afford to fly.'

Southwest's former CEO, Herb Kelleher, was not a normal chief executive either. He was routinely described as a character, charismatic, colourful and larger than life and was known for his love of cigars and whiskey. He imprinted his fun-loving personality on the business. His unconventionality as CEO extended to dressing up as Elvis for commercials (and as a leprechaun on St Patrick's Day); he smoked five packs of cigarettes a day and liked nothing better than to stay up all night partying; employees would invite him on hunting trips, never expecting him to come – and he would. He'd greet new employees by rapping (and curious readers can find the rapping CEO on YouTube).

But if he sounds nuts, he was also an excellent boss and regularly won plaudits as America's best CEO. He said things like 'A company is stronger if it is bound by love rather than by fear', and his staff really did love him. They showed their love with extraordinary productivity, which is one of the reasons Southwest has been such a success. Indeed, Kelleher's mix of big personality and business nous has led many to suggest that, while Southwest's model has been copied round the world, you can't actually learn that much from the man himself. The reason? He's unique – nobody else in the business world is quite like him.

Kelleher was born on 12 March 1931, near Camden, New Jersey. He was a good student, an impressive athlete and a student body president. After school, he went to Wesleyan University, where he studied English literature. He then went on to New York University School of Law. While at university he worked in the summer for Campbell Soup Company, where his father was General Manager. While at New York University, Kelleher lived in Greenwich Village. By all accounts, he was quite a fun guy and liked a party, which was why he chose this address. He said, 'I had a little apartment on Washington Square, and you could just open your door and entertaining people would walk in and you would have an instant party.'

After law school, he began as a clerk for a New Jersey Supreme Court justice. He then moved to Newark, New Jersey, and married a Texan. While visiting her family in San Antonio, he developed a liking for the place, in terms both of liveability and of the professional opportunities there. The couple decided to move to Texas, and he set up a law practice there. In 1966, a client of his, Rollin King, who had recently visited California, told him about PSA, the low-cost West Coast carrier. King believed that something similar could work in Texas. In 1967, the pair founded Southwest Airlines. Back then flying was still very much a high-end, high-margin business; people dressed up to fly. The pair's strategy was twofold. They would use cheaper secondary airports, rather than main hubs, and they would cut all the frills. Both would make flying cheap.

The idea for Southwest was supposedly sketched on a napkin. They drew a triangle described by Dallas, Houston and San Antonio; they would serve all three cities from a Dallas base. The airline, which was originally called Air Southwest, was incorporated in 1967, but did not actually start flying until 1971 because of regulation and litigation from rivals who hoped to strangle the fledgling business at birth (doubtless in the years to come they would wish they'd tried harder). The early 1970s were very difficult years – Kelleher has said that, during that time, 'We were just trying to survive day to day.'

In 1973, though, Southwest had its first profitable year, and the following year what was still a little local airline carried its millionth customer. In 1977, it carried its five-millionth and was listed on the New York Stock Exchange under the symbol LUV. The following year the President, Lamar Muse, stepped down, and Kelleher stepped up as interim CEO; four years later, he became permanent CEO. The airline continued to grow apace. In 1979, it added a service to New Orleans. In 1981, it celebrated 'a decade of love Southwest style', and in 1982, when Kelleher became permanent CEO, Southwest added further-flung destinations such as San Francisco, Los Angeles, Las Vegas and Phoenix.

The company also began to attract extraordinary plaudits. Its customers loved it, whether they were leisure passengers or cost-conscious businesspeople. Employees loved it and went the extra mile. Kelleher was cheerleader in chief for a business where everyone seemed to be enjoying themselves. In 1989, the airline earned a billion dollars. In 1990, it established a culture committee, because it was concerned about retaining its distinct corporate culture as it grew. In 1991 came its 20th anniversary of being airborne, and it celebrated '20 years of loving you!' with parties at its 32 bases. By the end of the year, it owned 124 aircraft and employed nearly 10,000 people. Between the late 1980s and the mid-1990s, the company more than tripled in size.

Soon afterwards, the airline expanded to the East Coast, but along with geographic expansion it also pioneered many innovative ideas. Its planes were all Boeing 737s, as having a single type of aircraft made maintenance and scheduling easier. It was the first to introduce ticketless flying and the first (major) airline to introduce online booking. The kooky stuff was everywhere too. Planes were killer whales. In 1993, when the airline acquired Morris Air, a Utah carrier, it staged a wedding. Kelleher challenged another CEO to an arm-wrestling match over the use of a slogan. Attendants joked as they went through the safety announcements. There is a well-known anecdote about how, after a particularly hard landing in Salt Lake City, the pilot announced, 'That was quite a bump and I know what ya'll are thinking. I'm here to tell you it wasn't the airline's fault, it wasn't the pilot's fault, it wasn't the flight attendant's fault... it was the asphalt!'

For all the headline-grabbing craziness, the biggest differentiator between Southwest and others carriers, both high- and low-cost, is the connection it has with its customers. To take just a recent example, low-cost carriers have started charging customers for luggage, often with a Byzantine system of rules and tariffs that seem designed to confuse the customer in order to raid their wallets. By sharp contrast, Southwest makes a big deal of flying bags free – and in an industry where many players' models seem ever more reliant on sneaky charges it is a big deal.

At the heart of all this was Kelleher and his belief in his staff. In 1994, a *Fortune* magazine article asked 'Is Herb Kelleher America's best CEO?' (Labich, 1994). The answer apparently was yes, as in 1998 Southwest was named *Fortune* magazine's best employer. Kelleher has always held that being a good employer is just a kind of enlightened self-interest. 'Employees', he explained in 2003, 'come first and if [they] are treated right, they treat the outside world right. The outside world will use the company's products again and that makes the shareholders happy.' In fact, Southwest is a very good place to work and, as well as Kelleher's bonhomie, Southwest pays generous salaries, and this in an industry that is known for exactly the opposite. The company even made a point of recruiting staff with a sense of humour.

In 1999, Kelleher was diagnosed with prostate cancer. He continued working throughout his treatment, which was ultimately successful. In 2001, he stepped down as CEO of the airline, although he remained Chairman. In 2008, at the age of 71, he relinquished this role after holding his 31st AGM. However, he remains an employee of the company until 2013, on a salary of $400,000 a year, and says he does whatever he's asked to do.

Of course, nutty or not, the ultimate test of a business is whether it makes money. Crazy people who make money are maverick geniuses; crazy people who don't are just crazy. By this yardstick Kelleher and Southwest have put in an outstanding performance. In 2010, Southwest was profitable for the 37th year in a row. In any industry this would be impressive – but in the airline industry it's doubly so, especially as the airline managed to make money in both the recent financial crisis and in the year after 9/11. The airline's share price rocketed between the late 1980s and the early 2000s and even now has not suffered as much as one might have expected.

Southwest does have a few critics, though. The airline was fined heavily in 2008 for lax safety and maintenance, and in 2009 a plane had to make an emergency landing in West Virginia when a football-sized opening in the fuselage led to the depressurization of the passenger cabin. Less seriously, in 2010, the film director Kevin Smith memorably lambasted the airline when it kicked him off for being too fat to fit in his seat. However, the consensus is much along the lines of one employee's comments on Amazon about the 1998 book *Nuts! Southwest Airlines' crazy recipe for business and personal success*, the staffer wrote:

> I have read the reviews about how this book is 'mushy.' I think maybe because they can't believe that a company this good really exists... I can safely say that the book does NOT exaggerate! The feel-good style emphasized over and over in the book is a reality. People care about each other. Every day (as shown in the book) everyone is made to feel valuable – and it makes you want to work harder, work smarter, and spread the LUV.

References and further reading

Bird, J B (2003) An entrepreneur for all seasons, *McCombs School of Business Magazine*, Spring/Summer

Freiberg, Kevin and Freiberg, Jackie (1998) *Nuts! Southwest Airlines' crazy recipe for business and personal success,* Crown Business

Kelly, Brad (2008) He gave Southwest its wings, *Investor's Business Daily*, 8 February

Koenig, David (2008) Kelleher steps down as Southwest Airlines chairman; he and client started business; employees give emotional send off, *Associated Press*, 22 May

Labich, Kenneth (1994) Is Herb Kelleher America's best CEO?, *Fortune*, 2 May

Southwest website, www.southwest.com

WATS (IATA)

Chapter Twenty Five
Andy Grove

The man who has been called the Henry Ford of microprocessors is also what might be termed first-generation Silicon Valley (with people like Steve Jobs and Bill Gates being second-generation and those from the dotcom boom onwards being third-generation). As such, Grove was all about hardware, not software. This sounds almost old-fashioned these days. But it isn't, and Intel's chips have had and continue to have as profound an effect on the world of technology as the Windows operating system or Apple's beautiful gadgets. In fact, you could easily argue that they're more fundamental. The ever shorter technology upgrade cycle is driven largely by Intel. New Intel chips appear far more frequently than new versions of Windows.

Grove himself – Intel's third employee and eventually its CEO – has an extraordinary life story and one that isn't a bad stand-in for the story of the 20th century. A Hungarian by birth, he survived the Nazis and fled his country for the United States, arriving a penniless immigrant. Entirely self-made, he rose to become one of the most influential men in technology – and later a hugely influential management thinker. He has authored a number of books, ranging from the bestselling *Only the Paranoid Survive* (1996) to *Swimming Across* (2001), his rather moving autobiography. Finally, he became a hugely important figure in the fight against prostate cancer. Yet in the world of big-ego US management he remains a very modest man.

Grove was born in Budapest in 1936 as András Gróf. He caught scarlet fever as a child, nearly died, and was left with significant hearing loss. During the Second World War, his father vanished, but he and his mother managed to evade the Nazis. At the end of the Second World War, the oppression and brutality of the Nazis were replaced by the oppression and brutality of the Russians; as he would reveal in *Swimming Across*, a Russian soldier raped his mother. Grove's father reappeared horribly emaciated from his time in the camps. Grove has said that it took him years to be able to talk about these events.

When the Russians crushed the Hungarian uprising in 1956, Grove and a friend made a break for the Austrian border. With the help of various people, he made his way across Europe and boarded a ship for the United States. When he arrived in New York in 1957, he was penniless and spoke no English.

As a Hungarian refugee Grove was awarded a one-year scholarship to study at New York's City College, washing dishes to support himself. He graduated in 1960, with a degree in chemical engineering. He then studied for a doctorate at the University of California, Berkeley. Around this time Grove realized that the future – and the big money – was not in chemicals but in electronics, so after graduating in 1963 he joined Fairchild Semiconductor, a pioneering integrated circuit manufacturer, as a researcher. Grove progressed up the ranks and became Assistant Director of Research and Development in 1967.

However, Fairchild was soon struggling and was about to experience a massive loss of staff. Two of these were Gordon E Moore (after whom Moore's law is named) and Robert Noyce. This pair left to found Intel in 1968. Andy Grove was the company's third employee. At the time, there was very little to the company: it wasn't much more than a business plan and a promise of funding. The idea was to make integrated circuits and memory chips – it was a promising field, but there was nothing especially groundbreaking about it.

Moore and Noyce had originally thought that Grove would look after the research side of things, but Grove soon decided that, despite his background, he was far more interested in manufacturing and that his real talent lay in industrial organization. What he wanted to do was to make the company's manufacturing as efficient as possible, and he soon earned a reputation for confronting problems head on and asking tough questions – and in a way that could seem rather brutal to those involved. Grove had two qualities that marked him apart from normal tough rationalizers. First, he was very good at articulating what he did – indeed, he had a knack for a catchy phrase, and ideas such as 'constructive confrontation' sounded rather good. Second, he was brilliant at industrial organization, and his streamlining of production processes, which were very crude by today's standards, resulted in a huge boost in profitability. The *Washington Post* described him as 'the drill sergeant at Intel'.

The 1970s saw the very first signs of the technological tsunami that resulted in the information revolution, the computerization of everything and the internet. Intel brought the first commercial microprocessor to the market in 1971, and the company's sales boomed. Its chips were the basis for the very early PCs of the 1970s. Although this was still very much a niche market, the company was starting to believe that this wouldn't long be the case and that these chips could have far greater applicability. It ploughed vast amounts into R&D. By 1979, the company was a big player and Grove was President, but the primary product remained memory chips.

In 1979 the company set out to establish itself as the microprocessor manufacturer of choice in a campaign called Operation Crush, as a number of new competitors had entered the market. Specifically, its goal was to win over IBM, which it managed to do, and with IBM using its 8086 chips it had the microprocessor market where it wanted it. However, even with this success it was still having to run to stand still. Its market remained one where prices were always going down. Rich competitors (for the barrier to new entrants was now a financial one) were snapping at its heels, and its memory chip market was being flooded by cheaper Japanese models. In the early 1980s, Grove decided to withdraw from this area of the market altogether and focus on microprocessors. Here the market had grown thanks to the IBM and its clones and, for the most part, it could dictate the pace. Nonetheless it was a bold step into the unknown.

It was here that Grove effectively became the prime mover behind the company. He was a firm believer in hard work and long hours – and kept a list of workers who arrived after 8 am. He was soon nicknamed 'the Prussian General', but was also a very good manager. Alongside the hard work was an ability to organize and motivate. There was also plenty of empowerment too – like many other great bosses, he left people to get on with things. As the 1980s progressed, the company realized that its chips were moving out of the office and into the home.

Grove became CEO in 1987. The market for chips continued to develop – and the pace of change speeded up exponentially. Every time Intel launched a new product, it was already looking beyond it, because soon the new product would be standard and the price that could be charged for it would fall. Moreover, although Intel was the market leader it had plenty of competitors to keep it on its toes. One of Grove's best-known aphorisms (and the title of one of his bestselling books) is 'Only the paranoid survive', and it's easy to see how he came up with it in a market where looking over your shoulder has to become second nature.

In 1989, Intel began to develop the Pentium chip, the successor to the 386 and 486 chips that were powering most of the world's computers; interestingly, that name, rather than 586, was chosen because the courts had ruled that the number couldn't be trademarked. The company struggled during the early 1990s recession, and Grove, ever the taskmaster, stipulated that all professional employees should work a 50-hour week on the same pay. By 1993, things were looking up. The Pentium was launched with the kind of fanfare more normally associated with new cars or hotly anticipated albums, an indication perhaps of how mainstream computers had become. The company spent a colossal amount on marketing (unheard of for what was essentially a component manufacturer) and introduced the famous 'Intel inside' jingle.

It all looked great, but the following year Grove made his biggest mistake, and his flagship chip caused the biggest headaches of his career. In 1994 a flaw was discovered in the Pentium P5 Floating Point unit by Thomas Nicely, a professor of mathematics at Lynchburg College. Grove responded first as an engineer would – pointing out that the flaw would barely affect anyone. At the time, he said, 'If you know where a meteor will land, you can go there and get hit.' This did not go down well with legions of home users, and he later admitted that he didn't understand that dealing with consumers was very different to dealing with people who understood how electronics worked. In the end, the company offered to replace the processors free of charge. The crisis eventually cost half a billion dollars – although there was a consensus that, in the long term, their grasping the nettle did their image quite a bit of good.

This aside, the 1990s were a very good decade for the company – it cemented its market lead, and its share price soared. Grove published the bestselling *Only the Paranoid Survive* in 1996, and the combination of an attractive, high-tech industry, managerial genius and a certain down-to-earth quality made Grove one of the superstars of management in the mid- to late 1990s. However, his astonishing success as a high technocrat was about to take a back seat to his health. In 1995, he was diagnosed with prostate cancer. Grove more than came clean about it. In fact, in May 1996, he was on the front page of *Fortune* magazine under the strapline 'Taking on prostate cancer'. In the piece he wrote:

> My secretary's face appeared in the conference room window. I could see from her look that it was the call I was expecting. I excused myself and bolted out of the room. When I stepped outside, she confirmed that my urologist was on the phone. I ran back to my office.

He came to the point immediately: 'Andy, you have a tumor. It's mainly on the right side; there's a tiny bit on the left. It's a moderately aggressive one.' Then, a bit of good news: 'There are only slim odds that it has spread.' The whole conversation was matter-of-fact, not a whole lot different than if we had been discussing lab results determining whether I had strep throat.

But what we were talking about was not strep throat. We were talking about prostate cancer.

His frankness about his disease only served to boost his profile and the esteem in which he was held. (His ghostwriter Catherine Fredman recalls: 'I asked, "Incontinence or impotence? That's what everybody wants to know." There was another pause and he gave me what I needed.') In 1997, he was named Man of the Year by *Time* magazine. It was in response to the interest shown in him after this that he started working on *Swimming Across* (published in 2001), which revealed a great deal of hitherto unknown material about his childhood.

Grove put the kind of effort into combating his disease that he had into running Intel. After doing huge amounts of research, speaking to numerous experts and carefully weighing up the odds, he underwent a relatively new kind of radiation treatment – and one that has worked so far. In 1998, he stepped down as CEO and President and became Chairman. This was a role he relinquished in 2005; he currently holds the title of Senior Advisor.

For a man who has overcome so many obstacles, Grove's tale has a sad coda though. In 1999, he noticed a tremor in his hand. Having survived everything from scarlet fever, to the Nazis, to prostate cancer, he now had Parkinson's disease. This time, he kept it quiet, revealing it publicly in 2006 in a biography. 'I did not want to become a poster child for yet another disease. I was so sick of being the first and last contact for prostate cancer', he says. 'Cancer you don't see. This thing makes me look like an old man. And I'm a vain guy.' That said, he is fighting it with exactly the same vigour with which he took on prostate cancer – and he has a fair amount of time left before things get bad, so, if anyone stands a chance of getting the better of Parkinson's, it's Andy Grove.

As for Intel, as with many tech companies, its share price has never quite regained the peaks it scaled in the glory years of the dotcom boom, but it has maintained its market share, which is not so different from what it was in the early 1980s. Even now, despite strong and sustained competition, it is number one in all its main markets, and its chips continue to drive the pace of technological change.

As an interesting footnote, it's perhaps worth noting that, by Silicon Valley standards – and by the standards of what he's achieved – Grove's fortune is relatively modest and measures in the hundreds of millions, rather than the billions. Indeed, throughout his life, he has been known as a man who eschews the normal trappings of CEO mega-wealth – the jets, the architect-designed mansions, the islands and so on. As he once told the *Wall Street Journal*, 'One position says you ought to put some effort into making sure that people know what you do. The opposite is, look, you'll never get 100 percent credit, so just do your stuff. Advertising your achievements will probably make you look like a jerk anyway. I lean toward the second view.'

References and further reading

Corcoran, Elizabeth (1996) Intel's blunt edge, *Washington Post*, 8 September
Corcoran, Elizabeth (1998) Intel CEO Andy Grove steps aside, *Washington Post*, 27 March
Dolan, Kerry A (2008) Andy Grove's last stand, 28 January
Gross, Daniel (1996) *Forbes Greatest Business Stories of All Time*, Wiley, Oxford, pp 246–65
Grove, Andrew S (1996) *Only the Paranoid Survive*, Profile Books, London
Grove Andrew S (2001) *Swimming Across,* Warner Books, New York
Intel, Biography: Andy Grove, www.intel.com
Parker, Ciaran (2006) *The Thinkers 50: The world's most important and influential business thinkers*, London Business Press, London
Rigby, Rhymer (2010) Ghosts and the corporate gurus, *Financial Times*, 22 February
Wallace, G David (2001) The struggle to become Andy Grove, *Businessweek*, 3 December

Chapter Twenty Six
Roman Abramovich

From a tragic and impoverished childhood spent in Russia's frozen hinterland to his current oil-lubricated billions, Roman Abramovich is probably the man who best epitomizes the new Russia. Whether on the London stage, flanked by a guard of minders, relaxing on his mega-yacht or buying major works of art as other people do newspapers, he is the living, breathing embodiment of what has happened since the fall of Communism and the rise of Russia's capitalist state. Like so much of the new Russia, he could easily have sprung, fully formed and powerful, from the pages of a John le Carré novel.

Strangely though, in the UK, he is probably best known as a tabloid staple, not because red-top readers are fascinated by Russian oligarchs, but because he is the owner of Chelsea Football Club – or 'Chelski' as it was inevitably rechristened after he purchased it. But even with this calling card, Abramovich has a past that is a shadowy and ill-documented place: it's easy to read 10 different accounts and come away with 10 different stories that differ quite noticeably. He's well known for being mysterious and powerful, and the power and mystery seem to feed off each other. He's notoriously media shy and very rarely gives interviews.

Anyone who knew Abramovich in his early years would never have imagined him as a billionaire playboy in London. He was born in 1966 in Saratov, a biggish city on the River Volga in southern Russia. His mother died when he was 18 months old, and his father was killed on a building site accident when he was four. In fact, the deaths of his parents were simply the latest instalments in a tragic family history, as his paternal grandparents had caught the eye of the KGB under Stalin. The family was torn apart, and the parents were sent to the gulags; only his maternal grandmother survived. Those looking for clues to Abramovich's extraordinary drive often point to this bleak backdrop.

Young Roman was adopted by a paternal uncle, who was an official in the oil industry, and his wife in Ukhta, an oil and gas town barely south of the Article Circle. They raised him as their own, and he only learnt that he was not their child when he was 16. Supposedly, upon discovering this fact, he took it in and never spoke of it again. The other close figure in his early years was his grandmother who had survived the gulag. Abramovich studied at the Industrial Institute in Ukhta and then worked for the Gubkin Oil and Gas Institute before going into the Army to do his national service.

After leaving the Army, he married his first wife. The couple were given a 2,000-rouble wedding present by her parents. Abramovich used this, trading on a local market, moving up the value chain and eventually trading pig farms. Communism was on its last legs, and Abramovich clearly had a bent for capitalism, although he was really no different to thousands of other traders who were too young to have had their entrepreneurial spirit ground down by Communism. But through his upbringing, Abramovich did have connections in the oil and gas industry, and he was learning to use these.

Soon, he was comparatively wealthy. He opened a tyre business in Moscow and moved into oil and gas trading, buying Russian oil very cheaply and selling it on the open markets for Western prices. In 1992 he was investigated over the theft of 55 rail wagons of gasoline, which was intended for a business in Moscow and which ended up in Latvia; the investigation moved to his home town and was then dropped. Over the next few years, Abramovich founded more businesses and moved his activities on to the international stage. He was now rich by even Western standards – but not seriously rich.

It was around this time that the privatization of Russian enterprises started. Workers in the state-owned businesses were given vouchers that could be exchanged for shares; many of them didn't have a clue what this meant, but Abramovich had been a practising capitalist since the mid-1980s. He understood the value of the vouchers and has been connected to schemes to buy them up en masse. His big break came in 1995, when he met Boris Berezovsky. He introduced Abramovich to the inner circle of Russian power – and Yeltsin.

Next came their crucial move. By the mid-1990s, Russia was almost bankrupt, and Yeltsin's administration was tottering. The solution was to sell off state assets to the 'oligarchs', as people like Berezovsky were now known, at rock-bottom prices; the quid pro quo would be loans to keep the government solvent. Yeltsin – and the oligarchs – also wanted to avoid a return to Communist rule, the former because he'd be out of power and the latter because their asset gains would be renationalized sharpish. Putting together a series of short-lived companies, for just over $100 million, Berezovsky and Abramovich bought the oil company Sibneft, which was worth over $2.5 billion. Like many other participants, Abramovich admits the assets were sold for a song, but he says the reason for this was that the risks (including that of a return to Communism) were so great. This may be a not entirely convincing explanation.

Next, Abramovich set his sights on the aluminium industry. This particular period was called the 'Aluminium Wars'. Abramovich emerged triumphant and unhurt. By 1996, he was so wealthy that he had become very close to Yeltsin and been invited to move into an apartment in the Kremlin.

Abramovich had a talent that Berezovsky didn't have though. He was charming and diplomatic. He made friends, whereas his former mentor made enemies. In 1999, Putin swept to power, and shortly afterwards Berezovsky left the country, having fallen foul of the authoritarian new president despite having helped him to power. However, while Berezovsky antagonized the new regime, Abramovich was made of more amenable stuff. He and Putin found common ground, and he became the person people were starting to call the 'stealth oligarch' and the 'oligarch from nowhere'.

In 1999, Abramovich stepped into politics – he became the Governor of a frozen and desolate region of the Russian far east called Chukotka, a region roughly the size of Germany with a population of just over 50,000. In fact the only thing the area had going for it was large (and largely unexploited) reserves of oil, gas and minerals. In 2005, he was appointed to a second term, which lasted until 2008. Although the province acted as a tax haven for Sibneft, Abramovich's two terms did see a significant improvement in the lot of ordinary people, and most of this came through Abramovich's investing billions of roubles of his own money.

For someone who has always guarded his privacy jealously, in 2003 Abramovich made a curious move. He bought the London football club Chelsea for £140 million – a move that guaranteed him a place in the spotlight. He said at the time: 'I love this game. I love this sport. I love this league. Why don't I get my own team?' He was prepared to spend to turn them into winners (which has yet to happen) and had the money to do so. The answer to a question posed by Chelsea fans about the source of Abramovich's wealth is that it came largely from the people of Russia. In a 2004 *Guardian* piece, an oil worker from Noyabrsk called Mikhail Karpenko was quoted as saying, 'he did scoop up the shares of those too poor and uneducated to appreciate their potential value. He did hustle thousands more out of their stake in Russian oil as the economy collapsed around them. He won. Russia lost' (Levy and Scott-Clark, 2004). This perhaps is a little black and white, as Abramovich's great fortune is in some ways a huge fluke. The 1990s in Russia were a crazy, chaotic time, and he happened to be the right person in the right place. His extraordinary wealth is in some ways an accident of history, and if he hadn't seized the opportunity someone else would have. That said, he has been considerably more careful about how he's managed his businesses than many other oligarchs and has managed to recognize that, in Putin's Russia, huge wealth buys you huge influence, but that there are lines you do not cross.

In the meantime, there are plenty of distractions. He has his mansions and his family, and in 2009 he launched his new yacht, the world's largest, which even has its own submarine. However, despite his high profile, he remains enigmatic, and much about him is unknown. Indeed, were it not for Chelsea, it's likely that much less would be known about him. One of his favourite sayings is purportedly 'Money loves quiet.' Insulated by his rows of bodyguards, public relations personnel and lawyers, it would seem that Roman Abramovich does too.

References and further reading

Buckley, Neil and Belton, Catherine (2007) Man in the news: Roman Abramovich, *Financial Times*, 7 December

Conradi, Peter and Lewis, William (2003) The tsar of SW6, *Sunday Times*, 6 July

Daily Mail (2005) Tortured past of Britain's richest man, 22 October

Kennedy, Dominic (2008) Roman Abramovich admits paying out billions in political favours, *Times*, 5 July

Kirby, Terry (2003) From Chukotka to Chelsea, 3 July

Levy, Adrian and Scott-Clark, Cathy (2004) He won, Russia lost, *Guardian*, 8 May

Levy, Geoffrey (2003) Shadowy tsar of Stamford Bridge, *Daily Mail*, 3 July

Lloyd, John (2000) The autumn of the oligarchs, *New York Times*, 8 October

Meek, James (2003) From Russia with £3.4bn, *Guardian*, 3 July

O'Connor, Brian (2005) Russian revolution – the billionaire oil baron who has shaken up Britain's social elite, *Sunday Telegraph*, 23 October

Stewart, Will (2009) Roman and the KGB file that unearths tragic family secret, *News of the World*, 20 December

Sunday Business Post (2010) Roman's empire, 2 May

Vander Weyer, Martin (2004) The winner of Russia's free-for-all, *Sunday Telegraph*, 31 October

Chapter Twenty Seven

George Soros

Saint or sinner? Ruthless speculator or philanthropist? Unacceptable face of capitalism or lefty activist with a peculiar philosophical bent? Outsider – as he likes to portray himself – or the ultimate insider? George Soros, the man who famously broke the Bank of England in the 1990s, is all of these things and many more.

Over his long career he has earned the hatred of any number of politicians (notably Norman Lamont and John Major, whose reputations he irreparably damaged) by attacking their currencies. His Open Society Institute, which he funds lavishly and which works around the globe, has led to charges of a God complex. He recently promised to give Human Rights Watch $100 million. The US Right despises him – indeed, he often funds organizations that seem diametrically opposed to what they want to do – but many in the former Eastern Bloc have a great deal of affection for him. Academics and politicians regularly scoff at his sorties into their fields, but sometimes he's right. As an investor, he has had a following whose devotion sometimes seems more suited to pop fans. Personally, he's often said to be rather charming.

Soros was born in Budapest in 1930 to an upper-middle-class family. His father was a lawyer with a strong interest in the artificial language Esperanto, and the family had a house on an island in the River Danube. They enjoyed an enviable lifestyle in a prosperous city with a rich cultural and intellectual life. Despite this, Soros has said that his father did not believe that all was as it seemed; Soros's father had been a prisoner of war in Russia during the First World War, and the experience gave him a great – and as it would turn out rather prescient – sense of foreboding.

In 1944, the Nazis arrived in Budapest. Soros said, 'My father was more than prepared. He knew what to do.' The family separated, and Soros's father paid an official in the Ministry of Agriculture to take his son in. Soros later described this as 'high adventure, like living through *Raiders of the Lost Ark*'. He also said that it laid the foundation for some of his later philosophical meanderings.

Soros's father's ruse worked, and the family survived. George is said to have had an early dabble in finance during the chaos after the war, trading in gold and jewellery as hyperinflation took hold.

In 1946, the Soviet Union began to take control of Hungary. While attending an Esperanto conference in the West, Soros defected. In 1947, he emigrated to England, where he worked as a railway porter and waiter, while studying at the London School of Economics (LSE). While at the LSE, he became very interested in the work of the philosopher Karl Popper, which made a strong impression on him. He became acquainted with Popper, wrote a number of essays for him, toyed with the idea of becoming an academic and even wrote a thesis called 'The burden of consciousness'. Soros graduated in 1952, but his attempts to become a philosopher went nowhere, and he found himself drawn to finance. He joined the investment bank Singer & Friedlander, where he worked in arbitrage, mainly in gold.

In 1956, Soros emigrated to the United States. He got a job with FM Mayer as an arbitrage trader and analyst. He covered European securities, which were far from most Americans' radar. Soros's second-in-command, Stanley Druckenmiller, said in 1988, 'The things George was doing 35 years ago have only come into fashion in the last decade here.' Soros himself said, 'No-one knew anything about [European securities in the early 1960s] so I could impute any earnings I wanted to the European companies I followed.' Soros's career took off. In 1959, he moved to Wertheim & Co, and in 1961 he became a US citizen. In 1963, he moved to Arnhold and S Bleichroeder, which was a leader in the field of foreign securities. Soros was an obvious fit and did well, becoming a Vice President. Interestingly, during this time, he continued to work on his philosophy, sending papers back to Popper at the LSE.

In 1967, he set up an offshore investment fund called First Eagle and then, in 1969, the Double Eagle Hedge Fund. His career really took off in the following year, when he founded his own investment fund called the Quantum Fund with Jim Rogers, another celebrated investor. At this point he still wanted to be a philosopher, and the idea was that trading might support this. As it was, the fund was to be an extraordinary success that would put Soros at the forefront of global investors. In 1981, the magazine *International Investor* said of Soros, 'As [Bjorn] Borg is to tennis, Jack Nicklaus is to golf and Fred Astaire is to tap dancing, so is George Soros to money management.'

For all this, Soros remained comparatively unknown outside the financial community and the business press. This would all change a decade later. In September 1992, he made the biggest and most successful bet of his life. Essentially he bet £10 billion that the pound was going to fall against the Deutschmark. His thinking was that the UK currency had entered the European Exchange Rate Mechanism (ERM) (a system designed to reduce exchange rate volatility in Europe) at too high a level and that its continued valuation at this rate was unsustainable. So, using Quantum and several other funds, he bet against it, converting his £10 billion into Deutschmarks.

Norman Lamont and John Major, the UK's then Chancellor and Prime Minister, had said they would defend the pound at any cost and that the pound would not leave the ERM (Soros would later say that the words did not carry conviction). They didn't quite get to 'any cost', but they did manage to spend £6 billion defending sterling. It didn't work. On 16 September, sterling was suspended from the ERM and effectively devalued. Major and Lamont were humiliated. Soros changed his Deutschmarks back into sterling and trousered a cool $1 billion. Many have said that to some extent, when Soros started saying the pound was overvalued, it became a self-fulfilling prophecy. Once it was known that Soros and the other speculators were shorting sterling, it was only a matter of time before sterling crashed. Soros's winnings were paid by the citizens of the UK – at about £12 a head.

After this, Soros was followed even more avidly than before by investment junkies and by and large continued his remarkable record. Towards the end, he did hit a couple of notable low notes. In 1998, he lost $2 billion in the Russian financial crisis. Curiously, this was an area he really was thought to have an inside track on – he believed the Russians had successfully made the transition from gangster capitalism to the more normal kind. They hadn't, and he lost out. He would later say he was deceived by his own belief in Russia. Now he will only say of the matter, 'I don't discuss Russia because I don't want to invest there.'

He also managed some exquisitely bad timing in the dotcom bust. He bet that tech stocks would crash, but made his move a year early, losing $700 million. He then went back into stocks that did crash, in March 2000; his total losses were around the $3 billion mark. At this point he announced his effective retirement from Quantum. Despite these troubles, his was an astonishing record. Had you invested $1,000 in the Quantum Fund when it started in 1970, by 2000 it would have been worth $4 million – equivalent to a 32 per cent annual increase lasting three decades, an astonishing track record.

Of course, a man like Soros was never going to retire quietly to look after his rose garden, and he had a second career to fall back on, which wasn't philosophy. He'd been an active philanthropist from the early 1970s onwards, but had been particularly interested in

Eastern Europe and had given heavily to promote democracy in former Communist countries. In all, Soros has given something like $6 billion to his various causes and now, after Gates and Buffet have made their enormous gifts, he is the fourth-largest philanthropist of all time (number three is Li Ka-shing). He has said, 'I don't like finding ways of spending large amounts of money. I consider it a chore. It requires a lot of effort which doesn't give me any satisfaction, so giving the money away (as opposed to spending it) gives me a lot of satisfaction.' He also became a very vocal opponent of the Bush administration and was often heard making statements such as 'President Bush is endangering our safety, hurting our vital interests, and undermining American values.'

This earned him the hate of the American Right – and probably accounts for some of the wilder rumours about him. Indeed, Soros became so demonized by the Right and so hated by the likes of Fox News that his support for Obama was very muted. He said this was because Obama wanted to be a unifier – and Soros recognized that he was a divisive figure. Even now, he is rarely out of the news, whether he's making his trademark pronouncements of doom or funding progressive causes. He's 35th on the *Forbes* (2010) list of the world's billionaires, with a cool $14 billion to his name. In fact, for all the fuss about newly rich hedge fund managers in the last decade, Soros remains the richest of them all and added another $1 billion to his wealth in 2009.

Strangely, in the end Soros may actually wind up with some of the intellectual recognition he craves. He's long been something of a doomsayer, but his latest work, *The New Paradigm for Financial Markets*, which came out in 2008, was a bestseller and earned him an invitation to testify in front of Congress. That said, most will remember him as one of the greatest speculators of all time and a man who had an incredible feel for the markets. He will also be remembered as a philanthropist and an activist of sorts and of course, in the UK, as the man who broke the bank, something he views as a tragedy. The philosophy, alas, will almost certainly remain an interesting footnote.

References and further reading

Bates, Daniel (2010) Billionaire financier George Soros hands $100m gift to U.S. human rights group, *Daily Mail*, 8 September

Clark, Neil (2003) The billionaire trader has become Eastern Europe's uncrowned king and the prophet of 'the open society'. But open to what?, *New Statesman*, 2 June

Deutschman, Alan (2001) George Soros, *Salon*, 27 March

Ellis, Charles D (2001) *Wall Street People*, vol 2, Wiley, Hoboken, NJ

Forbes (2010) The world's billionaires, 10 March

Freeland, Chrystia (2009) The credit crunch according to Soros, *Financial Times*, 30 January

PBS (2008) Bill Moyers journal, 10 October

Rieff, David (1994) The Soros touch, *Observer*, 16 January

Slater, Robert (2009) *Soros: The life, ideas, and impact of the world's most influential investor*

Soros, George (2008) *The New Paradigon for Financial Markets: The credit crisis of 2008 and what it means*, Public Affairs, US, NY

Steiner, Rupert (2001) Last mission of the man who broke the bank, *Sunday Times*, 15 April

Steiner, Rupert (2006) Bill Gates is just a figurehead, I am actively engaged, *Spectator*, 15 July

Sylvester, Rachel and Thomson, Alice (2009) The man who broke the bank says that we're facing global meltdown, *Times*, 28 March

Thompson, Susan (2008) Business big shot: George Soros, *Times*, 22 January

Tyler, Christian (1993) Private view: the man who broke the Bank of England, *Financial Times*, 2 January

Chapter Twenty Eight
Akio Morita

A t the end of the decade that has seen the iPod sweep all before
it and become so popular that it is more normal to say iPod
than MP3 player, it's worth remembering that we've been here
before. In 1979, Sony launched the Walkman, which was the world's
first mass-market portable stereo cassette player. The Walkman was
a sensation and changed the way we listen to music. Like the iPod
it dominated its market utterly, and in every sense it was the iPod's
predecessor.

It was also an indication of the massive global power of the Japanese
electronics giant Sony, which in the 1980s (as today) was a maker
of consumer electronics that targeted the upper end of the mass
market. Nowadays, of course, Sony is one of the better companies
churning out consumer electronics, but its market is a mature one,
and there are plenty of competitors who make similar products.
However, in the 1980s it was much more. The company and its
iconic co-founder Akio Morita were also symbols of Japan's post-
war economic success, its commitment to quality, and the economic
threat that these appeared to pose to the United States. Indeed, if
you substitute China for Japan, and the iPod for the Walkman,
2010 and 1980 don't seem so far apart.

While Morita personified the post-war Japanese economy for many outside Japan, he was also something of a maverick within Japan, a deeply conformist country that gave the world the expression 'The nail that sticks out is hammered down.' Morita often swam against the current and challenged conventional wisdom. He was also one of Japan's keenest internationalists. For this reason, in his heyday, he was almost certainly Japan's best-known businessman – and probably the only one most people in the wider world would have recognized.

Morita was born in 1921 in Nagoya, in central Japan. His parents were wealthy, and he was the heir to a sake brewing dynasty that traced its roots back to the 16th century. As he was a first son, it was assumed that he would work for the family firm, but his family's wealth worked against his destiny. As a boy, he became fascinated by the imported phonograph his parents owned – one of the first in Japan. He began building his own electronic devices, including a radio receiver and another phonograph of his own devising. This led him to study physics at Osaka University, rather than economics as his father had hoped. In the Second World War, he served in the Japanese Navy on a research group whose remit was to be 'original and audacious thinkers'. While working on weapons, he met Masaru Ibuka, an engineer 13 years older than him, who was to become the technical genius behind Sony. Ibuka would also help persuade Morita's father to allow him to pursue a career in electronics, rather than sake.

In 1946, in a Tokyo devastated by the Second World War, Morita and Ibuka founded a firm called Tokyo Tsushin Kogyo (Tokyo Telecommunications Engineering Corporation); most of the $500 seed capital came from Morita's family. The pair, then aged 25 and 38, set up shop in a bomb-damaged department store, with 20 staff, aiming for a business where technical expertise and innovation were celebrated and encouraged. Resources were scarce in post-war Japan, and the pair had to improvise. Cellophane – rather than stronger plastic – was used for tape, and the original magnetic powder that held the recorder was cooked up in a frying pan. The tape recorder went on sale in 1950 to no real interest at all. It wasn't until Morita showed court stenographers how useful it could be that it started selling. This, Morita has said, taught him a valuable lesson about the need to create markets for new products whose uses may not be immediately apparent.

The company's next product was the one that would make its name and fortune. The transistor had been developed by Bell Laboratories in the United States, and in 1952 Morita bought the licensing rights for $25,000 despite considerable resistance from the powerful Japanese Ministry of International Trade and Industry (MITI). This decision was probably the single greatest he made, not least because the transistor's applications were considered very limited at the time. In 1955 the company produced the first commercial transistor radio. In 1957, it produced the world's first pocket-sized transistor radio. In fact, the pocket-sized claim was a bit of a stretch – the company actually had to issue its salesmen with shirts with oversized pockets in order for the radios to fit. With the success of the radio, the innovations really started. In 1960, the company developed the world's first all-transistor TV and, in 1967, the Trinitron colour TV. The TV's technology was developed in order not to infringe restrictive US patents, but it resulted in a sharper picture that gave it the edge. Trinitrons would be desirable televisions for decades.

The company wasn't innovating just in terms of its products. In insular post-war Japan, it was also looking outward. In 1958, a decision was taken to change the company name, which by now was well known in Japan. This didn't go down well with Japanese consumers, but Morita defended the decision, saying that it was necessary because the company had its eyes on other markets and needed a name foreigners wouldn't struggle with. Sony was chosen (from the Latin *sonus*) as something easy to pronounce and remember. In 1960, the company founded Sony Corporation of America. In a Japan that was still very conservative, Morita was a cosmopolitan internationalist. In 1961, Sony became the first Japanese company to offer US depositary receipts, which allowed the company to raise capital beyond Japan.

In 1963, Morita went one better, upping sticks and moving to New York with his family for a year in order to gain a better understanding of how Americans lived and worked. In 1966, he wrote a book called *Never Mind School Records*, which challenged Japanese employment practices, saying that companies should focus on employees' abilities, not their qualifications; it caused quite a stir. In the early 1970s, Sony built a factory in the United States and, later on, it even had Western directors on its board. Morita himself socialized with US businesspeople and, again a rarity back then, spoke pretty good English.

The company's startling record on innovation continued, although it made a notable bad call in the late 1970s. Sony had developed video recorders in 1965, although it didn't launch its Betamax for home use until 1975. However, it refused to license the technology to others. This led a group of other Japanese companies to develop VHS, which eventually harried Betamax, a system many thought technically superior, into oblivion. However, Sony soon bounced back. In 1979, the company developed what was arguably its most iconic product – the Walkman. Again many doubted it, while Morita was its champion. Sony produced a stereo that let you shut the world out wherever you were, which was perfect for the selfish decade – 230 million were sold.

By the 1980s, Sony had plants all over the world. In the early years of that decade, the company, in conjunction with Philips, developed the CD, which by 1990 had effectively signed the LP's death warrant. The CD's use was later expanded as a recordable medium for computers. Sony launched the first consumer camcorder. At the end of the decade it made what was widely seen as a blunder when it bought Columbia and Tri-Star Pictures (it is thought to have overpaid). Nonetheless, it became one of the world's biggest record companies. The innovations continued too – it was part of the DVD Consortium, it invented the MiniDisc (which was huge in Asia, but never embraced fully by the West), and the first PlayStation appeared. By many measures, for most of the 1990s, Sony was the best-known brand in the United States.

But the 1990s were to be the end of the line for Morita. In his late 60s, and with an astonishing legacy behind him, he'd finally been embraced by the Japanese industrial establishment with which he'd always had a rather fractious relationship. He was set to become Chairman of Keidanren, the country's most influential business organization, but in 1993, during a game of tennis, he suffered a cerebral haemorrhage. In 1994, when Sony announced its Hollywood flop, he resigned as Chairman. Despite rehabilitation his condition worsened and, in 1999, he died aged 78 of pneumonia in a Tokyo hospital. Shortly before his death *Time* magazine listed him as one of the most influential business geniuses of the 20th century. The company's former Chairman, Nobuyuki Idei, said, 'It's not an exaggeration to say that he was the face of Japan.'

This perhaps was the most contradictory aspect of Morita. Many in Japan had long suggested that he might be happier in the West than he was in his own country. He just seemed so un-Japanese. In a country where, even now, ostentation is frowned upon, he had a corporate jet and a helicopter, he was an avid sportsman, he hung around with celebrities and he appeared in an Amex ad. He had the temerity to criticize Japanese business culture, saying that it was too insular. He even called on his country to open its rice market.

Interestingly, his son has said that this was all essentially a façade, and others have suggested that he was in fact deeply uncomfortable with being the face of Japan for foreigners. This 'act', it's been suggested, was a reaction to the psychological effects and national inferiority complex a generation of Japanese suffered after losing the Second World War. Whatever the case, foreigners certainly liked it: they bought enough of Sony's products to make it a global giant, and Morita's international activities brought him international recognition. He received the Albert Medal of the Royal Society of Arts in the UK, the French Légion d'honneur and numerous other awards from dozens of countries.

References and further reading

Economist (2008) Guru: Akio Morita, 16 November

Financial Times (1999) Obituary, 4 October

Guardian (2009) Akio Morita – the man who gave the world the Sony Walkman, 5 October

Nahan, John (1999) Asian millennium – Akio Morita 1921–1999, *Far Eastern Economic Review*, 25 November

New Straits Times (2000) Akio Morita, 10 September

Pollack, Andrew (1999) Obituary, *New York Times*, 4 October

Purcell, William (1999) Sony founder led electronic revolution, *Australian*, 5 October

Sony website, Biography, History, www.sony.com

Times (1999) Obituary, 4 October

Tsuruoka, Doug (2009) Akio Morita made Sony shine, *Investor's Business Daily*, 23 September

General sources

BBC
Businessweek
Economist
Financial Times
Forbes
Fortune (especially the rich list and list of billionaires)
Guardian
New York Times
Observer
Sunday Telegraph
Sunday Times
Telegraph
Time
Times
Wall Street Journal
Wikipedia

Index